PRESCHOOL BIBLE LESSONS

by
Myrna Loehrlein and Dawn Nylin

illustrated by
Elizabeth Nygaard

Cover by Jeff Van Kanegan

Shining Star Publications, Copyright © 1990

A Division of Good Apple, Inc.

ISBN No. 086653-541-1

Printing No. 987654321

Shining Star Publications
A Division of Good Apple, Inc.
1204 Buchanan St., Box 299
Carthage, IL 62321-0299

By the grace God has given me, I laid a foundation as an expert builder, and someone else is building on it. But each one should be careful how he builds. For no one can lay any foundation other than the one already laid, which is Jesus Christ.
I Corinthians 3:10, 11 NIV

The purchase of this book entitles the buyer to reproduce student activity pages for classroom use only. Any other use requires written permission from Shining Star Publications.

All rights reserved. Printed in the United States of America.

Unless otherwise indicated, the King James Version of the Bible was used in preparing the activities in this book.

DEDICATION

For the children

of Lovely Lane Preschool

TABLE OF CONTENTS

To the Teacher/Parent 4

Home and Family
    August and September* 5

Life Changes
    October and November* 23

New Beginnings
    December and January* 41

Community Helpers/Stewardship
    February and March* 58

Growing Things
    April and May* 77

Joy and Celebration
    June and July* 89

Award Certificates 95

*These months are only suggestions.

TO THE TEACHER/PARENT

God made us—unique, priceless, and capable. Whatever the activity, concept, or skill you choose from *Preschool Bible Lessons*, the one pervasive theme is "God has made us each to receive and share His love."

Here is a resource of child-tested activities based on sound early childhood education principles, from which you can choose those best suited to your children and your program.

There are no patterns for you to copy, no lengthy preparations to be made, few pieces for you to cut out. These ideas center on young children and the things *they* can do. The product of their efforts should never be the goal. The emphasis should always be on the process of growth and discovery and the nurturing of capable learners who can know and share God's love.

Use *Preschool Bible Lessons* to fill out or offer variety to an already good program. Or, you may choose to use the units presented herein to structure an entire year of Bible-based study. You, the preschool teacher/parent, will know the best way to use these fun-filled lessons. Any way you choose, I know that these quality early childhood education principles and the theme of receiving and enabling the sharing of God's love will help you guide children toward a greater understanding of themselves and their world as a part of God's plan.

HOME AND FAMILY
August and September

Objectives 6
Crafts
   Home and Family 8
   House and Address 8
   Family Puppets 9
   Orange Corn Starch 9
   Emotion Mask Puppets............9
   I Am Special Book 10
   Family Portraits 11
   Mirror Picture 11
Learning Games
   My Family Can 12
   Silly Orange.....................13
   Which One Is Different?..........13
   Who Lives Here? 14
   Build a House 14
   Emotions 15
   Follow the Leader 15
Snacks 16
Show-and-Tell
   Family Photos 17
   Family Mementos................17
   Pictures of Child's House 17
   A Family Member................17
   A Family Pet 18
   Mementos of Family Activities 18
Field Trips
   Neighborhood Walk 19
   Nature Center Walk..............19
Visitors
   Members of Families............19
Finger Plays . . . and Songs
   I Am Special 20
   Give Yourself a Hug 20
   There Was a Family.............21
   Songs You Probably Know 21
Books and Resources................22

Objectives for Home and Family Unit

Children will be able to explain, draw, play or otherwise demonstrate:

VALUE OBJECTIVES

1. Healthy male or female roles knowing that both sexes can show love and anger, have good ideas, be leaders and followers

2. That each family member is as important as any other family member knowing that all people are valued because they are God's creation

3. That family structures differ

4. That home is a place where people cooperate so that all may grow

5. God has planned a home for everyone

6. Exploring ideas is good

SKILL OBJECTIVES (3 to 4-year-olds)

A. To participate in a group activity for a short time—about 10 minutes

B. To make a comfortable transition from mother or other caretaker to the preschool environment

C. To care for one's own things (jacket, craft to take home, etc.) with minimal assistance

D. To be familiar with the location and proper use of preschool equipment

Shining Star Publications, Copyright © 1990, A division of Good Apple, Inc.

E. To recognize and name the color orange

F. To name the main body parts

G. To practice low-level large and small muscle skills

SURVIVAL SKILL

H. To know the first and last names of self, mother, and father

SKILL OBJECTIVES (5 to 6-year-olds)

A. To participate in an extended group activity for a longer time—up to 20 minutes

B. To enter into preschool environment by caring for personal belongings, promptly finding and engaging in an arrival-time activity

C. To use preschool equipment creatively but with respect, putting it away appropriately

D. To classify objects and make sets (sorting and set building)

E. To name most body parts including specific parts such as "ankle" and "wrist"

F. To practice higher level small and large muscle skills

SURVIVAL SKILL

G. To know home address

CRAFTS

Home and Family

Concept   Each family member is important.

Skill   Family Names

Child is given a paper on which an outline of a house has been drawn. The child pastes simple cutouts of his/her family in his/her house and draws their faces. Teacher writes the first and last names of each family member. Child dictates names if possible, or teacher may attach a note asking parents to help child learn first and last names of family members.

House and Address

Concept   God has planned for homes.

Skill   Address

Child draws picture of his/her own house. Teacher writes child's address on picture. Child dictates address if he/she knows it or teacher may write it and attach a note asking the parents to help the child learn his/her address.

Family Puppets

Concept Each family member is important.

Skill Motor Skills
Body Parts

Child is given circles or ovals of paper. Child draws his/her family members, one on each piece of paper. Child may choose to draw either faces or more complete bodies. Child pastes pictures to Popsicle sticks to make puppets.

Orange Corn Starch

Concept Exploring

Skill Color Orange

This may not be considered a craft since no product results, but it is a very pleasant way to work with the color orange. Mix a box of cornstarch with a little water and color it orange. Experiment with various quantities of water until you get the consistency you like. Let the children just play in it; it is a great tactile experience.

Emotion Mask Puppets

Concept Males and females know how to show emotion.

Skill Motor Skills
Body Parts

Large ovals cut of sturdy paper with a generous hole left for looking through. Child draws various emotional faces on as many masks as he/she chooses: happy, sad, mad, surprised, etc.

Variation: Child may make emotion mask puppets if he does not like the idea of wearing a mask.

I Am Special Book

Concept Each family member is important.

Skill Motor Skills

This book may be sent home for parents to add to throughout the project, or kept at preschool for teacher to make the additions and send home when complete. It may include some or all of the following:

> drawings around hands or feet
> picture of self and family created by child in fall and again in spring
> child's measurements
>   on a leaf for fall
>   on a flower for spring
> "All About Me"-story told by child about himself/herself to teacher; child may add pictures.

The general format could include:

My name is _____.

I am _____ years old.

I live with _____.

I have a pet _____. I also like _____.

What I like about preschool is _____.

Don't forget to include your own ideas in this very special personal book.

Shining Star Publications, Copyright © 1990, A division of Good Apple, Inc.

Family Portraits

Concept   Family structures differ.

Skill   Motor Skills

Child draws picture of family members and may dictate a brief story about family (names, ages, jobs, etc.). Let child draw similar picture in the spring. It is fun to compare size and placement of family members.

Mirror Picture

Concept   Each family member is important.

Skill   Motor Skills

A small hand mirror is made with construction paper and either aluminum foil in center or white paper on which child draws a picture of himself/herself. Teacher may print around the rim "Look who is at preschool."

Notes and Ideas

LEARNING GAMES

My Family Can...

Concept   Each family member is important.

Skill   Group Activity
Motor Skills

Children use simple felt figures to represent family members. As they put a figure on the flannel board, they are to tell one thing that family member can do very well.

Variation: Children may "act out" the things family members do. These may be things like: give a hug, make someone laugh, eat something made especially for them, cook, go to work, accept kisses, etc.

Silly Orange

Concept   Exploring ideas is valuable.

Skill   Group Activity, Color Orange, Classify

Use the color orange to make simple drawings of things that are usually orange and things that usually are not orange. Hold them up one at a time so that the group can respond "really orange" or "silly orange." Be sure to have some items that are really silly, like an orange banana, bunny rabbit, etc.

Variation: Children can pull a drawing from a bag and show it to the group, or children can take turns responding.

Which One Is Different?

Concept   Exploring

Skill   Group Activity, Classify

Looks Different
   Put two or three matching or similar items on flannel board or on floor in front of the children. Put on one more item that is different. The children, either as a group or one at a time, tell which one is different. As they correctly identify the different one, they may hold it for the rest of the game. Make the differences more or less obvious depending on the children's abilities.

Sounds Different
   Fill pairs of old pill bottles or other small opaque containers with a variety of items like sand, pea gravel, salt, beads, corn, water, etc. Give two matching bottles and one different bottle to a child. Child shakes bottles, listens for and identifies the one that is different.

Smells Different
   Using pairs of baby food bottles or other small containers, place a cotton ball in each. On the cotton ball, place various scents like perfume, vinegar, lemon or banana extract, pickle juice, alcohol, etc. Children use these as they did the bottles in "Sounds Different" above.

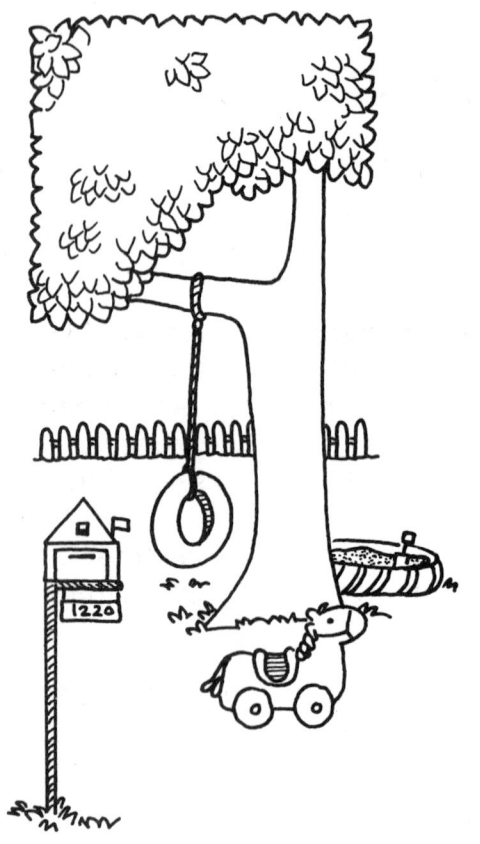

Who Lives Here?

Concept   God has planned homes.

Skill   Group Activity

Teacher describes one child's home one feature at a time. Tell things like:
- color
- yard features
- names of adults or others living there
- near-by features (example: a fence, fire hydrant, street light, etc.)
- architectural features (example: a fireplace, back porch, stairs, etc.)
- play items in the yard
- street address (if the child knows it)

Build a House

Concept   God has planned homes.
Families Differ

Skill   Group Activity
Motor Skills

Use pictures, drawings, or models to discuss the various kinds of houses in which families live (example: house, apartment, mobile home, etc.). Children tell group what kind of house they live in (teacher should accept what children describe even if it is inaccurate). Group uses materials provided by teacher to build a preschool house. Materials provided might include:
- cardboard cartons
- sheets
- a card table
- rope strung across the room or area

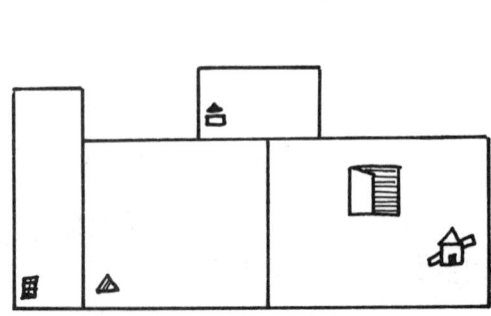

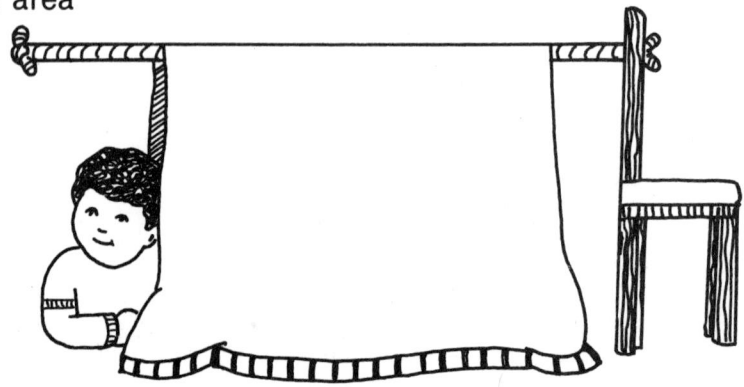

Emotions

Concept Males and females express emotions.

Skill Group Activity
Classify

Make simple drawings of faces showing emotions like happy, scared, surprised, mad, sad, etc. Acquaint the children with the drawings so they understand what each is meant to represent. (This step is especially helpful if your drawings are as simple as mine, but the children always seem to catch on.)

As children are shown drawings a second time, encourage them to make faces to match the emotions represented on the cards.

Variation: A child makes a face and the group chooses the matching drawing telling which emotion is being represented; or, the teacher tells a one or two sentence story illustrating an emotion, the child chooses the drawing of the emotion expressed by the story and names the emotion.

Follow the Leader

Concept Males and females can be leaders and followers.

Skill Group Activity, Large Muscle

Children take turns being leader wearing a man's hat, a woman's hat, or a child's hat.

Variation: The teacher may be the leader wearing the various hats. This game can be a traveling game or stationary action game in which the leader hops, stoops, etc., and the players follow his/her lead.

SNACKS

Concept   Exploring (tastes) is valuable.

Skill   Group Activity

Motor Skills (if child assists in preparation)
Color Recognition

orange sections or slices
American or cheddar cheese
macaroni and cheese (the kind from a mix comes out more orange)
carrots
Orange Julius
sweet potatoes
pumpkin
raisin/carrot salad

Note: Please avoid orange gelatin, sherbet, or other artificially orange and sweetened foods. There are plenty of tasty, naturally orange foods to choose from.

SHOW-AND-TELL

Show-and-Tell has a value that is consistent throughout this curriculum. It is, of course, a time when children gain and refine listening skills, speaking skills, and grow in language use. In this curriculum, it's also a time when the child learns that he/she is an important, valued, respected part of our community. The child learns that the others in the community are equally important, valued, and deserving of respect. It is a time when the children can see that even though each of us is different, we are all a part of God's family and valued for that reason. It is important for the teacher to use this time with intentionality, to communicate with her attention and attitude toward each child that he/she and his/her comments are unquestionably the most important thing happening in the preschool at that moment.

Each show-and-tell suggestion has a value of its own, and these will be noted separately.

Family Photos

Concept   Family structures differ.
Home is a place to cooperate and grow.

Family Mementos

Value   Each family member is important.

These may include a child's baby cup or spoon, a birth announcement, parents' marriage certificate or wedding pictures, etc.

Pictures of the Child's House

Concept   God has planned homes.

A Family Member

Concept   Each family member is important.
Family structures differ.

Yes, bring Grandma, Brother, Sister, etc., as a show-and-tell item!

A Family Pet

Concept   Family structures differ.
Home is a place to cooperate and grow.

Children often think of pets as full-fledged family members. A pet provides an occasion to emphasize that cooperation of caregivers is essential to the well-being of the pet.

Mementos of Family Activities

Concept   Each family member is important.
Family structures differ.
Home is a place to cooperate and grow.

These might include a *TV Guide*, picnic basket, fast food containers, camping equipment, games, books shared, etc.

FIELD TRIPS

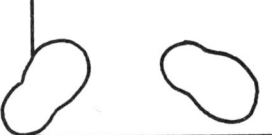

Concept God has planned for homes.

Skill Group Activity
Motor Skills

Neighborhood Walk

Take a walk in the neighborhood to view students' homes and the "home" of the preschool.

Nature Center Walk

Concept God has planned for homes.

Skill Group Activity
Motor Skills

If a nature center or wooded area is available, visit it to observe the various homes of the animals living there.

VISITORS

Concept Family structures differ.
Exploring ideas is good.

Skill Group Activity

Members of various kinds of families:
   singles living alone
   grandparents living with children and grandchildren
   a couple
   a family of parents and children
   a single-parent family
   a family with an "extra" member—uncle, aunt, foster child, etc.

FINGER PLAYS ...AND SONGS

"I Am Special" (tune: "Frere Jacques")

Concept   Each family member is important.

Skill   Group Activity

I am special, I am special.
Look at me, look at me.
Someone very special, someone very special.
Yes, it's me, yes, it's me.

You are special. You are special.
Look at you, look at you.
Someone very special, someone very special.
Yes, it's you, yes, it's you.

"Give Yourself a Hug" (tune: "Turkey Trot")

Concept   Exploring concepts is valuable.

Skill   Group Activity
Motor Skills
Body Parts

Pat on your head, cover up your eyes
Wiggle your ears, twink on your nose
Pinch on your cheeks, pull on your chin
Rub your tummy, and pat your knees.

Reach for your nose, twink on your nose
Pinch on your cheeks, pull on your chin
Rub your tummy, and pat your knees.
Give yourself a hug, and blow a kiss to me.

(Do the motions suggested by the words.)

"There Was a Family . . ."

Concept Each family member is important.

Skill Group Activity
Motor Skills

There was a family had a girl (boy)
And _____ (insert child's name)
was her/his name-o.
Stand up _____, Stand up
We're glad you're here today.

Songs You Probably Know—
"Hokey Pokey"
"If You're Happy and You Know It"
"Head and Shoulders, Knees and Toes"

BOOKS AND RESOURCES

Bible Stories

    The Prodigal Son—Luke 15:11-32
    Martha and Mary—Luke 10:38-42
    The Boy Jesus Lost in the Temple—Luke 2:41-52

Books

Brown, *The Important Book*, Harper & Row.

Cohen, Miriam, *Will I Have a Friend?* Lillian Hoban, illus., Macmillan, 1967.

Fisher, Aileen, *Best Little House*, N.Y.: Thomas Crowell Co.

Heide, Florence, *Who Needs Me,* Minneapolis, MN.: Augsburg Publishing House.

Keats, Ezra Jack, *Peter's Chair*, Harper & Row, 1983.

Linville, Barbara, *God Made the One and Only Me*, Heaston, Claudia, illus., P.O. Box 15337 Lakewood Station, Denver, CO 80215, 1976.

Miles, Betty, *House for Everyone*, Jo Lowery, illus., Knopf, 1958.

Skorpen, Liesel Moak, *We Were Tired of Living in a House,* N.Y.: Coward-McCann, Inc.

Tangvald, Christine, *Me, Myself, & I*, illus., Elgin, IL: David C. Cook, 1985.

Tangvald, Christine, *My Own Special Body*, illus., Elgin, IL: David C. Cook, 1985.

The Warm Hug Book, 6820 Auto Club Road, Minneapolis, MN 55438: Bethany House.

Watson, Switzer, Hirschberg, *Sometimes I Get Angry and Sometimes I'm Afraid,* Racine, WI, Golden Press, N.Y., or Western Publishing Co., Inc.

LIFE CHANGES
October and November

Objectives 24
Crafts
    Leaf Creatures 26
    Bouquets on a Page 26
    Leaf Stained Glass..............27
    Leaf Rubbings...................27
    Tombstone Rubbings 27
    Thank-You Notes to God.........28
    Thank-You Notes to Others 28
    Indian Leather Scroll 28
    I Remember Pictures 29
    Mini Bouquets...................29
    Halloween Crafts 29
    Lasting Impressions 30
    Pet Rocks 30
    Carton Caterpillars 30
Learning Games
    Leaping Leaves! 31
    Make an Indian Village 31
    Flannel Board Pilgrims..........32
    Obstacle Course 32
    What Do You See?..............33
    What Do You Hear?.............33
    Workplace 33
Snacks 34
Show-and-Tell
    Memory Memento 36
    Memory Photo 36
    Signs of Fall....................36
    Thank-You Things 36
    Something Brown 36
Field Trips
    Visit to an Apple Orchard 37
    Autumn Leaf Walk 37
    Visit a Farm 37
    Visit a Tombstone Manufacturer ...38
    Visit a Cemetery 38
Finger Plays . . . and Songs
    Apples 39
Books and Resources..............40

Shining Star Publications, Copyright © 1990, A division of Good Apple, Inc.

Objectives for Life Changes Unit
(including Death and Dying)

Children will be able to explain, draw, play or otherwise demonstrate:

VALUE OBJECTIVES

1. Change is an important and ever-present part of life

2. We can show love through helping, sharing, trusting

3. Making careful choices is important

4. Part of life in a positive way

5. Learning to say good-bye is important

6. We have much to be thankful for

SKILL OBJECTIVES (3 to 4-year-olds)

A. To practice saying please and thank you appropriately

B. To recognize when people are sad, mad, and happy, and begin to know how to express those emotions

C. To experiment using art media, paint brushes, finger paint, play dough, etc.

D. To recognize and name the color brown

E. To become aware of the special characteristics or particular objects, etc.

F. To continue practicing skills introduced in earlier units

SURVIVAL SKILL

G. To know where parents work, either home or workplace

SKILL OBJECTIVES (5 to 6-year-olds)

A. To practice please, thank you, and other courtesies

B. To recognize emotions, sad, mad, happy, surprised, lonely, frightened, and express them appropriately

C. To experiment with art media, paintbrushes, finger paints, play dough, markers, crayons, etc.

D. To know and name basic shapes (circle, square, triangle, rectangle, oval)

E. To become aware of the special characteristics of particular objects, etc.

F. To continue to practice the skills introduced in earlier units

SURVIVAL SKILL

G. To know home phone number

CRAFTS

Leaf Creatures

Concept   Death and Life

Skill   Art Media
Body Parts

Choose a leaf collected on a class walk or supplied by a teacher. Maple or oak leaves with deep jagged edges work well. Glue leaf to a large (12" × 18") piece of colored construction paper. This is a good time for the child to practice using small dots of glue. Child may finish picture by adding arms, legs, facial features, and other decorations of his/her choice.

Bouquets on a Page

Concept   Death and Life
Life Changes

Skill   Art Media

Choose from a variety of dried grasses and flowers gathered on a class walk or teacher may supply them. Fold construction paper or wallpaper at center and cut a vase. Arrange a bouquet of dried materials on background paper. Glue the "vase" over the bouquet.

Leaf Stained Glass

Concept Death and Life

Skill Art Media

Choose from a variety of autumn leaves gathered on a class walk (or teacher may supply them). Use leaves immediately or press under heavy books or other weight to prevent curling as they dry. Child arranges leaves inside a waxed paper "sandwich". With adult, child irons the paper with iron on low setting. Child folds a piece of construction paper in half and cuts out a square "c." When paper is unfolded, there is a frame for his picture. Staple leaf "sandwiches" to frames and display on window.

Leaf Rubbings

Concept Life Changes

Skill Art Media

Place a leaf under a piece of plain light-colored paper and rub the paper with a crayon. Leaves with prominent veins and stems work best. Try using the side as well as the tip of the crayon, one or several colors, or colored chalk. If you use colored chalk, spray the product with hair spray to set it. You may want to tape the leaf and paper to the table for younger children.

Tombstone Rubbings

Concept Death and Life

Skill Art Media

Locate a cemetery with tombstones with interesting carvings. You may be surprised at the variety available. Talk with the children about good cemetery manners and respect for this important place. Let children choose tombstones of interest to them. Help them tape large pieces of paper over the stone and rub with a crayon to transfer the design to the paper. Back at preschool, mount the rubbings on colored paper. Bright colors work well for this activity.

Thank-You Notes to God

Concept Thankfulness
  Show Love

Skill Courtesies
  Art Media

Talk with the children about the things they are especially glad that God has made and given us. Ask each child to think about one thing that they are especially thankful for. You may want to disallow choices of toys and other commercially available possessions. You may want to concentrate on nature, people, etc. If you do, the children may need considerable help identifying these items.

Once the children have decided on the thing they want to express thanks for, let them draw or paint a picture about that thing. Let them dictate a short story or title for their picture; write it for them, and attach it to the picture. Enclose the picture in a folder with the words "Thank You, God for . . ." or something similar on the front.

Thank-You Notes to Others

Concept Thankfulness
  Show Love

Skill Courtesies
  Art Media

Similar to above except the note is addressed to parents or others important to the child.

Indian Leather Scroll

Concept Thankfulness

Skill Courtesies
  Art Media

Let each child tear one side out of a large grocery bag and draw Indian designs or other designs of his/her choice on the brown paper with permanent magic markers. When the art is finished, let the children crumble it into a tight ball. Smooth out the wrinkled paper and rub it with brown shoe polish. The art work will resemble painting on leather. Be sure the children understand that Indians did not have paper and sometimes used pieces of leather to write or draw on.

I Remember Pictures

Concept   Death and Life
              Saying Good-bye

Skill   Art Media

In the lower right corner of a piece of drawing paper, make a simple drawing of a child's head. Above the head, draw a "balloon" of the type used in cartoons to show what a character is thinking or dreaming. The child fills in the child's "head" with a picture of himself/herself and fills in the cartoon balloon with a picture about someone who has died or moved away. The child should be encouraged to talk about his/her picture and dictate a short story or title for the teacher to write on the paper.

Mini Bouquets

Concept   Life Changes

Skill   Art Media

Choose from a variety of dried grasses and flowers gathered on a class walk or supplied by the teacher. Cut to very short stems (1-3 inches). Using medicine cups, nut cups, bottle caps, or other small containers, let children mix a small amount of plaster of paris or patching plaster to a stiff consistency in the container. No matter how these bouquets are arranged, they look attractive.

Halloween Crafts

Concept   Exploring

Skill   Art Media
              Body Parts

Make Halloween "masks" by letting the children draw hair, ears, a bow tie, etc., on the edge of a paper plate from which they have cut the center. Place a Popsicle stick or cardboard stick on the bottom so the children can hold their "masks" and see them in the mirror.

Make Halloween costumes from grocery bags. Invert the bag and cut a hole in what was the bottom for the child's head; cut holes on either side just below the former bottom for the child's arms. Let the child decorate the costume with paint, pasted collage materials, markers, etc.

Lasting Impressions

Concept Life Changes

Skill Art Media

Similar to crayon rubbings but in a different medium. Find leaves with particularly evident veins and stems. Lay them on Play-Doh or clay and use a rolling pin to put leaf impressions into the dough or clay. The impressions can be dried and left as is or painted.

Pet Rocks

Concept Death and Life

Skill Art Media

Following a discussion of what is alive, what is dead, and what has never been alive (more appropriate for older children), the children can make the following "pets."

Each child brings in a rock, or class may find them on a nature walk or field trip. Child makes a creature of his/her rock by adding glue-on wiggly eyes, a yarn or leather thong tail, painting on wings, etc.

Carton Caterpillars

Concept Death and Life
Life Changes

Skill Art Media

The caterpillar to butterfly metamorphosis is a dramatic example of a life change. The children can make a part of this transition by making caterpillars using sections of egg cartons for the body (pressed paper egg cartons work the best, but are difficult to find). To the sections of cartons, add chenille wire legs and antennae, eyes, paint stripes, etc.

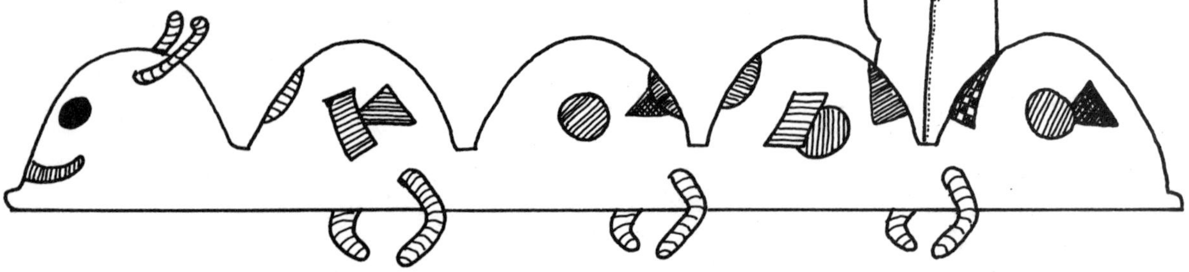

LEARNING GAMES

Leaping Leaves!

Concept Life Changes

Skill Motor Skills

Build large piles of leaves and use them for jumping in, rolling in, leaping over, or just sitting in. Let the children rake leaves or make the piles or even ask parents to dump their leaf bags in the preschool yard!

Make an Indian Village

Concept Thankfulness
Show Love

Skill Group Activity
Art Media

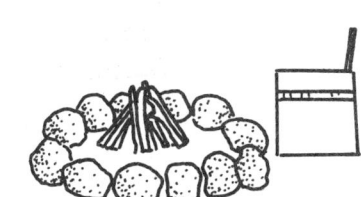

Set the scene by reading books showing how Indians built their houses and villages. Read or talk about the first Thanksgiving and how the Pilgrims and Indians celebrated it together.

Build the village by letting the children gather (or bring in) rocks to arrange in a fire circle. Arrange twigs to represent a fire. Make a tent by draping blankets over a frame. Add a boat or "canoe" made from a large box and painted by the children. Complete the scene with dolls and kitchen utensils brought from the housekeeping corner.

Flannel Board Pilgrims

Concept   Thankfulness

Skill   Observing
                Art Media

Make a set of felt or flannel Pilgrim and Indian figures for the children to dress. Talk about what the children have been seeing in stores as decorations for the holidays. Explain that the Pilgrims and Indians dressed differently from the way we do today; indeed, they dressed differently from most of the other people of their day. The Pilgrims dressed simply to express their religious convictions against excessive adornment; the Indians dressed in ways that denoted the tribe to which they belonged.

Allow the children to dress the flannel figures. This would be good for some appropriate costumes for dress-up play.

Obstacle Course

Concept   Exploring

Skill   Motor Skills
                Color Brown

Build an obstacle course using tables to crawl under or over, boxes to jump off of, a balance beam or masking tape strip for a "bridge," large balls to roll from one place to another as the child moves along (at the destination, the child throws the ball back to the next child or into a large basket), beanbags to balance on the head, shoulders, outstretched hands, etc., as the child walks. Use your imagination and the materials at hand.

Make the obstacle course a color learning experience by putting brown construction paper, carpet squares, or other brown obstacles within the course. The children must avoid the obstacles as they move through the course.
Or put brown tickets along the way. The children collect all their brown tickets as they move through the course. When all the tickets are collected, they may paste them on a ticket puzzle to complete a picture.

What Do You See?

Concept   Exploring

Skill   Observation

In a manner similar to the game "Riddles, riddles, ree, I see something you don't see," teacher chooses an object and gives clues such as color, function or other physical attributes (is round, has legs, is heavy, etc.). Once children have become comfortable with the game, let them take turns describing the mystery object.

Difficulty of this game can be increased by using items that are not visible to the players.

What Do You Hear?

Concept   Exploring

Skill   Observation

Begin by asking the children to lie still in the rest area and listen for the sounds they can hear from there. Identify them and their source. After the listening session, make a picture chart of the sounds, their source, and the location of the listening experience. Follow up this experience with trips to other nearby "listening posts." Try a variety of locations, a busy corner, in a park, near a school, in the quietest room of your building. Make picture charts for all your listening experiences. Compare them to discover the sounds you heard in more than one place, or sounds that are unique.

Workplace

Concept   Live Today

Skill   Observation

Make it a special event by having the children dress as their parents do when they go to work and/or bring an object their parents need to work. We have had great fun with this day. We have had everything from homemakers to car painters. This day gives the children and their parents a good opportunity to talk about where Mom and Dad work. After "Work Day" at school, you can review the parents' workplaces with each child individually or play a game with the information. At the beginning of the circle, the children can stand. As the teacher names a workplace, all children with a parent who works there may sit down.

 # SNACKS

Concept	Exploring tastes is valuable.
Skill	Group Activity
	Large and Small Muscle
	Courtesies

Sauteed and lightly salted pumpkin seeds
   (Use seeds from the pumpkin you carve for Halloween.)

Popcorn
   (Can be related to Pilgrims learning from the Indians when discussing Thanksgiving.)

Apple Wheel Sandwiches
   (Make cheese and/or peanut butter sandwiches using circular apple slices, made across the fruit, instead of bread.)

Applesauce
   (May be cooked or raw; in either case, be sure to use the peel, too. To make raw sauce, simply puree in a blender with a little sugar and lemon juice.)

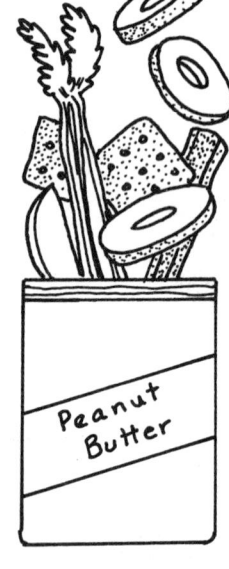

Comparison Snacks
   (Fresh fruits and their dried counterparts may be eaten and compared as part of the death unit.)

Indian Pudding (Recipe follows)

Cranberry Salad (Recipe follows)

Brown Snack Ideas

Peanut Butter
   (On crackers, bread, apple slices, in celery, etc. Use care with peanut butter, it can cause choking when eaten in sizeable "blobs".)

Gingerbread and gingerbread people

Whole wheat cinnamon toast

Pumpkin Custard
   (Simply bake a pumpken pie without the crust!)

Peanut Butter

1. Measure 1 cup peanuts
2. Pour in blender, cover, blend on high for five seconds
3. Add: 1 tablespoon oil, blend on high ten seconds. Switch to low for forty-five seconds.
4. Remove from blender

Eat immediately or store in refrigerator.

Yield: 1 lb. unshelled peanuts = 1½ cups shelled = ¾ cup peanut butter

Cranberry Salad

2 cups ground cranberries
½ cup diced apples
½ cup pineapple tidbits

Stir together and chill before serving

Indian Pudding

¼ cup liquid shortening
1 cup cornmeal
1 cup whole wheat flour
¼ cup molasses

¼ cup maple syrup
4 teaspoons baking powder
1 cup milk
3 beaten eggs

Combine ingredients
Pour into 9" pan
Bake 400° F, twenty minutes

SHOW-AND-TELL

Memory Memento

Concept Life Changes

A toy or favorite possession of a chosen adult that the adult enjoyed as a child.

Memory Photo

Concept Death and Life
Saying Good-bye

A photo of a relative or friend the child has known but who has died or moved away. If none of these apply, a photo of a friend or relative the child knows but does not see very often because they live far away.

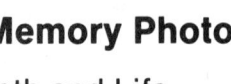

Signs of Fall

Concept Life Changes

Leaves, dried flowers and grasses, fall clothes, fall sports equipment, a fall calendar page, harvest materials . . .

Thank-You Things

Concept Thankfulness

Pictures or objects we can thank God for.

Something Brown

Concept Color Brown

Children bring objects or pictures of objects that are inherently or almost always brown.

FIELD TRIPS

Visit to an Apple Orchard

Concept   Life changes

Skill   Group Activity
                Courtesies

Visit an apple orchard to point out the changes in the trees and fruit in the fall. Notice workers picking and packing apples, the care with which the fruit is handled, any care given the trees, the surrounding vegetation which gives signs of autumn.

Autumn Leaf Walk

Concept   Life changes

Skill   Group Activity
                Motor Skills

Walk in the school neighborhood to view and experience autumn leaves, their colors, crunch, abundance, variety. Collect many samples to be used in craft projects. If you are lucky enough to find big piles, be sure to play in them. (Appropriate attention must be given to safety and respect for personal property, of course.)

Visit a Farm

Concept   Thankfulness

Skill   Group Activity
                Observation

Visit a farm to view signs of harvest. A general farm is good for relating to Thanksgiving activities, a pumpkin farm is good for relating to Halloween.

Visit a Tombstone Manufacturer

Concept Death and Life
Choosing

Skill Group Activity
Art Media

The children will be fascinated by the grinding and polishing processes. Plan carefully for safety, of course. Let the children choose favorites and touch as much as possible.

Visit a Cemetery

Concept Death and Life

Skill Group Activity
Motor Skills
Art Media

Visit a cemetery to view and touch tombstone carvings. Note the variety and beauty of the decorations and the beauty of the setting. Use the opportunity to practice respect for individual graves and the area as a whole. Try to go on a beautiful day so the children can enjoy the overall beauty of the area. Do some tombstone rubbings (see page 27).

FINGER PLAYS ...AND SONGS

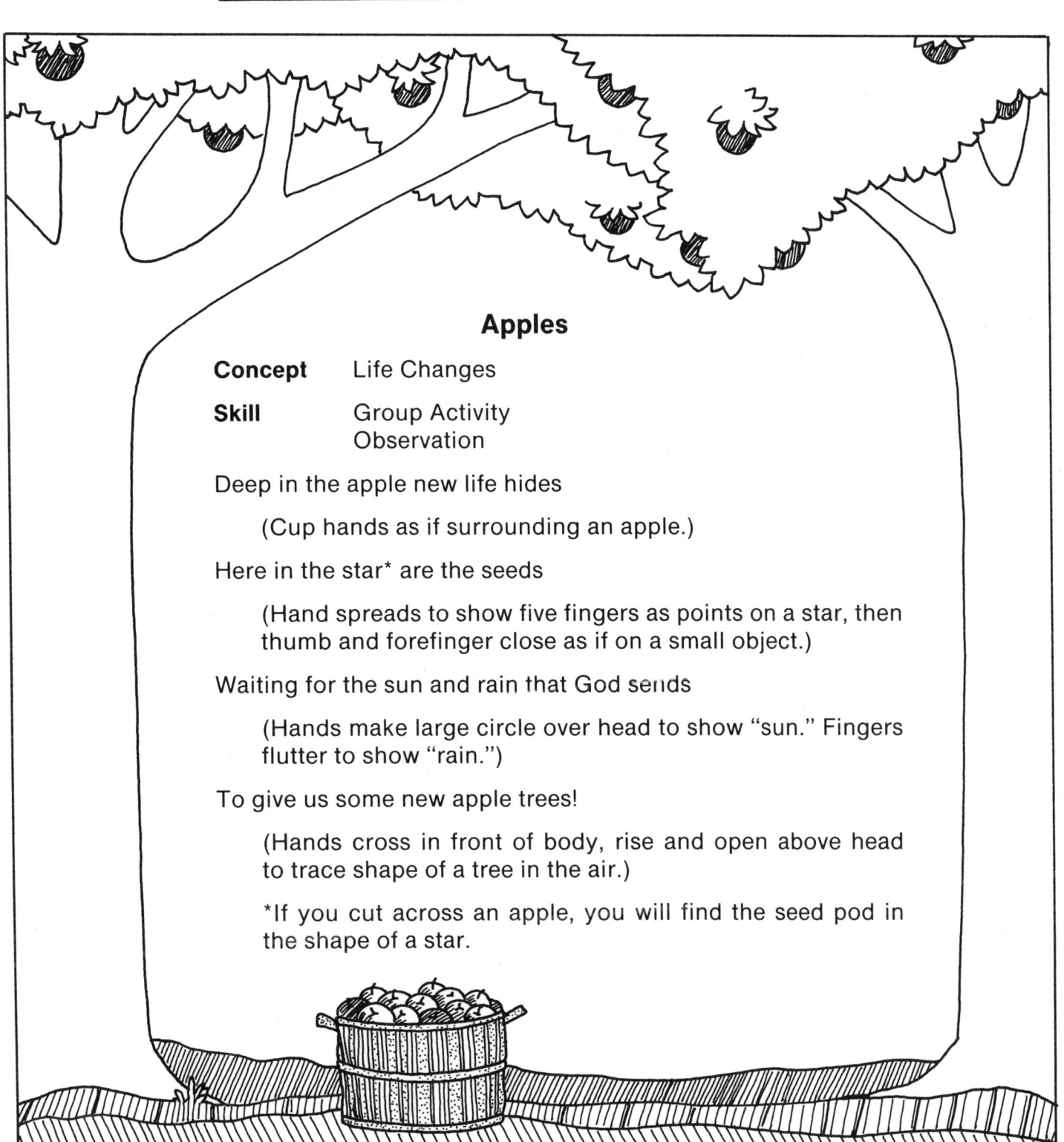

Apples

Concept Life Changes

Skill Group Activity
Observation

Deep in the apple new life hides

(Cup hands as if surrounding an apple.)

Here in the star* are the seeds

(Hand spreads to show five fingers as points on a star, then thumb and forefinger close as if on a small object.)

Waiting for the sun and rain that God sends

(Hands make large circle over head to show "sun." Fingers flutter to show "rain.")

To give us some new apple trees!

(Hands cross in front of body, rise and open above head to trace shape of a tree in the air.)

*If you cut across an apple, you will find the seed pod in the shape of a star.

BOOKS AND RESOURCES

Bible Stories

    Jesus Raises the Little Girl—Matthew 9:18-26

Books

Anderson, Phoebe M, *Mr. Red Ears*.

Clifton, Lucille, *Everett Anderson's Good-Bye,* Holt, Rinehart, and Winston, 1983.

DePaola, Tomie, *Nanna Upstairs, Nanna Downstairs*, Putnam, 1973.

Fassler, Joan, *My Grandpa Died Today,* Human Sciences Press, 1971.

Stiles, Norman, *I'll Miss You, Mr. Hooper*, Random House/Children's Television Workshop, 1984.

Viorst, Judith, *The Tenth Good Thing About Barney*, Atheneum, 1975.

Zolotow, Charlotte, *Janey*, Harper & Row, 1973.

_____ *My Grandson Lew*, Harper & Row, 1974.

Records

Rogers, Fred, *A Place of Our Own*, "There Are Many Ways to Say I Love You," "Wishes Don't Make Things Come True" (death and life), Family Communications, Inc., 4802 Fifth Ave., Pittsburgh, PA 15213.

Palmer, Hap, *Getting to Know Myself*, "Change," Educational Activities, Inc., Freeport, NY 11520.

Alsop, Peter, *Wha' D' Ya Wanna Do?* "My Brother Threw Up On My Stuffed Toy Bunny" (learning to say good-bye), "No One Knows For Sure" (death and life), "I Am a Pizza" (emotions), Flying Fish Records, 1304 W. Schubert, Chicago, IL 60614.

NEW BEGINNINGS
December and January

Objectives 42
Crafts
   Bird Feeders 44
   Christmas Goodies 45
   Christmas Chains 45
   Wood Scenes 46
   Tree Candles....................46
Learning Games
   Is This a Stranger? 47
   Hammer Stump 48
   911 48
Snacks 49
Show-and-Tell
   Christmas Tokens 50
   Color Blue 50
   Things of Winter.................50
   Christmas Memories 50
   Christmas Past 50
   Carpentry Share 51
   Future Plans 51
   Really Strong 51
   Tools 51
Field Trips
   Carpenter Shop or Wood Shop 52
   Winter Nature Trail 52
   Gift Collecting/Distributing 53
   Nativity Tour 53
Visitors 54
Finger Plays . . . and Songs
   Baby Jesus 55
   Christmas Finger Play 56
Books and Resources..............57

Objectives for New Beginnings Unit

VALUE OBJECTIVES

1. To become aware of God's gift of life to us through the birth of Jesus

2. To celebrate Christmas with joy and sharing instead of commercialism

3. To appreciate the day at hand free of the negatives of yesterday

4. To feel confident about tomorrow

5. To understand that God works through families, including children

6. To see that what seems weak may actually be very strong

SKILL OBJECTIVES (3 to 4-year-olds)

A. To rote count to 10

B. To count three objects

C. To identify three basic shapes (circle, square, triangle)

D. To classify "same and different"

E. To recognize and name the color blue

SURVIVAL SKILL

F. To know and be able to use properly "911" emergency number

SKILL OBJECTIVES (5 to 6-year-olds)

A. To rote count to 20

B. To count ten objects

C. To recognize and identify five basic shapes (circles, square, triangle, rectangle, oval)

D. To classify by a single characteristic—color, size, etc.

E. To gain proficiency in the use of scissors

SURVIVAL SKILL

F. To beware of strangers

CRAFTS

Bird Feeders

Value God's Children
 Confidence
 Live Today

Skill Motor Skills
 Shapes

We do a carpentry project each year as we talk about Jesus growing up in a carpenter shop. This is one of our favorites.

Give each child a square of scrap lumber, 1" × 6" × 6" works really well, but whatever you have available will do. Add four rectangles about 1" wide and cut to fit each side of the square. Help the children sand the lumber until it is reasonably smooth. Then, help them glue and nail the rectangles around the edge of the square to form low sides on the feeder. Help them drill 3 or 4 holes spaced around the perimeter for fastening the hanging chain. They can screw eyes into the holes and attach chain or simply hammer staple nails through one link of the chain and into the square. The children may then paint or otherwise finish the surface of the feeder, or it may be left unfinished. A little bag of bird seed to get the feeder started at home is a nice touch.

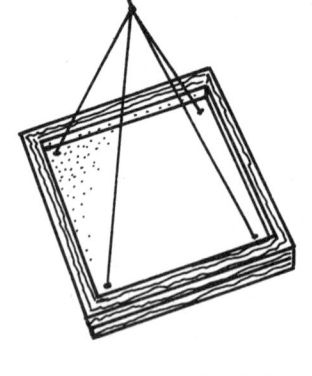

Note: This project often takes us two weeks or more, but the children love it; their feeders always come out serviceable if not artistic, and it gives us good experience with some of the tools Jesus may have used as he was growing up.

Any kind of simple bird feeder will help teach the values listed above and some of the skills. We like this one because it fits well with our carpentry theme.

Christmas Goodies

Value   Christmas
            God's Children

Skill   Motor Skills
            Shapes
            Object Count

In an effort to maintain nutritious eating habits while celebrating Christmas with joy, we enjoy making the following snacks.

Mix cream cheese with a few diced red Marischino cherries and a little of the juice to flavor and color the cheese. Mix another batch of cream cheese with a few green cherries and a little of their juice. Children spread the cheese mixtures on fresh, light whole wheat bread. Use appetizer cutters to cut squares, circles, triangles. Object count can be practiced by giving the children a particular number of each shape to cut. Children can serve these snacks to parents or other guests at a Christmas coffee or tea.

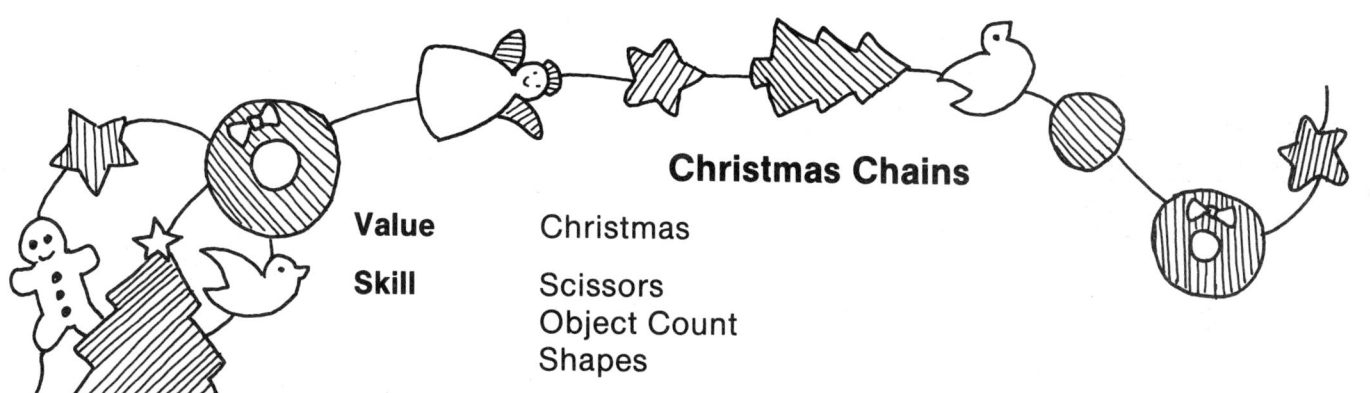

Christmas Chains

Value   Christmas

Skill   Scissors
            Object Count
            Shapes

Children trace and cut basic shapes out of Christmas colored construction paper, wallpaper, or wrapping paper. Children glue these shapes onto sturdy string by squeezing a line of glue onto the back of their shape and laying the string into it. All of one child's shapes should be glued onto one piece of string. The strings can be tied together to form one long chain or can be displayed separately. The Christmas tree is a good place to display these. Be sure the child's name is on at least one of the shapes on his/her section of the chain so it can be returned to him/her when the chain is disassembled.

This project can be used to learn about Christmas symbols by using these symbols instead of geometric shapes: candles, stars, simple tree shapes, wreath shapes, bells, simple angle shapes.

Wood Scenes

Value   Christmas

Skill   Shapes

Cut rounds from a 4"-8" log. A slice 1½"-2" thick and cut on the bias is just about right. The children may sand and seal these rounds in accordance with carpentry activities or they may leave them "natural." Have a variety of items available for the children to choose from and glue on to create a miniature scene on their round. Dried moss from a craft store or florist is a good background. You can add miniature animals, small rocks, tiny evergreen trees, foil or blue paper ponds, epsom salt flakes for snow, etc. It is hard to make one of these that is unattractive. These make very nice Christmas gifts.

Tree Candles

Value   Christmas

Skill   Scissors

Children decorate a bathroom tissue tube with Christmas colors or symbols they draw on paper, cut out, and paste on. Children cut a flame from yellow or gold paper and glue it onto the top of the tube to make a "candle." Cut a ring from one end of another tube and glue it to the outside of their "candle" so it can be slipped over the end of a Christmas tree branch. These "candles" will stand up on your tree. They are especially nice when lights are not used on trees for safety reasons.

LEARNING GAMES

Is This a Stranger?

Value Confidence

Skill Strangers
Classify

Have a variety of photos of teachers, aids, parents, your building staff, others the children might see and know. Include photos of pleasant looking people whom the children do not know. Each child is given a picture, he/she shows it to the group, and decides whether it is a stranger. If the child decides it is not a stranger, the child may tell who the person is, not necessarily by name. If the child decides correctly, he/she may keep the photo until the end of the game. If he/she decides incorrectly, he/she may have one more try. (The teacher may want to make the second try an easily identified photo.)

Once the children are proficient at identifying strangers, this game can be extended by playing a "What if" game. "What if this person offers you a piece of candy?" "What if this person offers you a ride in his/her car?" The answers will differ depending on whether the person is a stranger, family member, staff member, etc.

Note: Be sure to point out that a person who is a stranger to one child is not necessarily a stranger to another child.

Hammer Stump

Value Skill Development

Skill Large Muscle
Real Strength

During the time you are talking about tools and work in a carpenter shop, have a stump available for the children to hammer nails into. A stump works better than sawn lumber because it is sturdy, doesn't require a work bench, is relatively portable, and often the nails go in easier because of the grain of the wood at the cut surface. The children enjoy it and it is great practice for large muscles and eye-hand coordination. Just be sure to have light hammers and a great supply of short nails with very large heads. Demonstrate how to hammer a nail so children will not hit their hands with the hammer.

911

Value Confidence

Skill 911

Play a "what if" game. "What if no one is home and you get hurt?" "What if you get lost and can't find anyone to help, but you see a telephone?" "What if you get scared and can't find Mom or Dad?" One answer to these three "what if's" is call 911.

Practice on a large phone model letting children punch and dial (the children may need to use either kind of phone in an emergency). Practice on a real phone (with the receiver down, of course).

Be sure to include some situations in which the answer is not 911. Example: "What if you are hungry and Mom is in the backyard?"

SNACKS

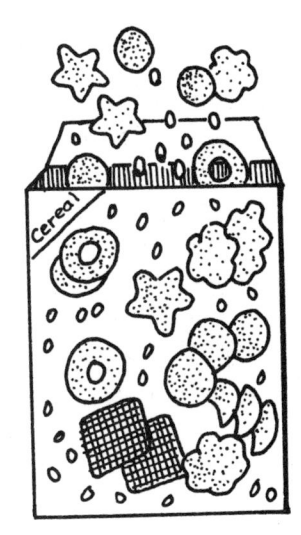

Snacks

**See note about snacks in snack section, Unit 1, page 16

Value   Skill Development
            Live Today

Skill   Shapes
            Classify
            Same/Different
            Color Blue

Cereal Mix
  Be sure to include a variety of shapes. The children may describe their identifying characteristics as they eat.

Shaped Crackers and Cheese
  Be sure to include a variety of shaped crackers and cheese cut into a variety of shapes. The children may identify the shapes as they eat.

Food Jesus May Have Eaten
  Dried fruits, pita breads, matzos, olives, goat cheese. These may be used in a variety of ways either to create a sweet snack or combined with other foods to make small sandwiches, etc.

Blue Snacks
  Blueberry muffins, blueberry pancakes, blueberry yogurt, blueberries with milk.

White Snacks
  Milk, bananas, coconut (try serving pieces of fresh coconut after you and the children have cut it open), popcorn.

SHOW-AND-TELL

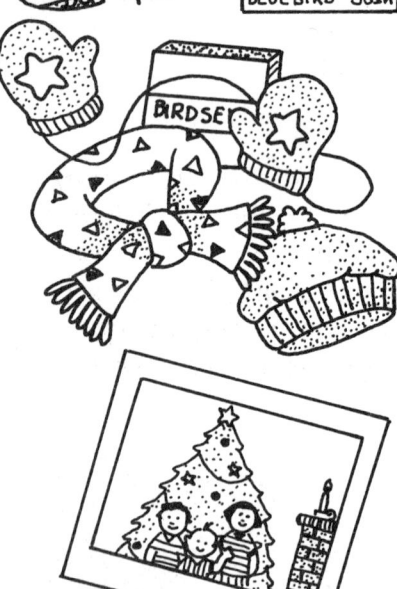

See Show-and-Tell Note—Unit 1

Christmas Tokens

Value Christmas

Review the symbols you have been working with: star, nativity scene figures, bells, candles, wreaths, Christmas trees, etc. Ask each child to bring something they use at their house just at Christmastime that has one of these symbols on it.

Color Blue

Skill Color Blue

Anything blue.

Things of Winter

Skill Observation

Anything the child sees or uses at home in the winter but at no other time.

Christmas Memories

Value Christmas
        God's Children
        Live Today

A picture of last year's Christmas activities.

Christmas Past

Value Christmas
        God's Children
        Real Strength
        Live Today

A picture or memento of a Christmas one of the child's parents enjoyed as a child.

Carpentry Share

Value   New Life
God's Children

Explore what Jesus might have played with as a child by bringing a toy or other plaything made out of wood.

Future Plans

Value   Confidence
Live Today

A token of something the child and his/her family are planning to do in the near future. It could be something as mundane as a hairbrush or other grooming tool that the child uses every day, or something more unique like a travel brochure, or something in between like an ad for a pizza parlor the family expects to visit in the near future.

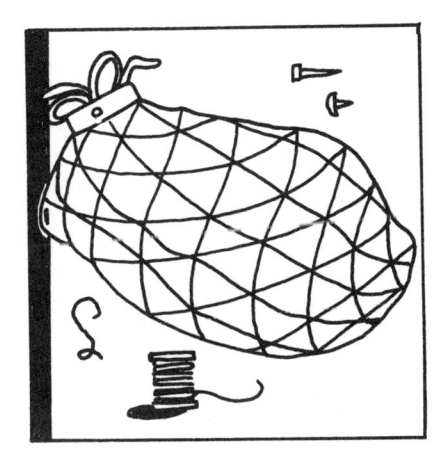

Really Strong

Value   Real Strength

Something that looks weak but is really capable of holding quite a load. It could be a Christmas ornament hook, a piece of fabric, a smaller sibling or friend, a mesh shopping bag, etc. The children can have fun with this one by experimenting with the various objects to see just how much they can hold.

Tools

Value   God's Children

Any tool that Jesus might have used in Joseph's carpenter shop. These will, of course, be non-power tools.

FIELD TRIPS

Carpenter Shop or Wood Shop

Value   New Life

Skill   Observation
Group Activity
Large and Small Muscle

We have had most memorable visits to our local high school wood shop. Our children were paired with the high school students to experiment with simple carpentry tools. They might sand, use a vise to hold their materials, try a brace and bit to make a hole in a scrap wood block, even see what happens when a simple oil finish is applied. The children then take their wood projects home and are ready to apply some of these skills in a more structured wood project at preschool.

Note: It is always a toss-up on which students enjoy and gain the most from these experiences, the preschoolers or the high schoolers.

Winter Nature Trail

Value   Live Today

If you had a chance to get to a nature trail or park in the fall, this is a good time to make a return visit. If you did not get out in the fall, go now, and let the children make some careful guesses about how the area is different now from what it was in the fall. It is not necessary to evaluate and/or correct the children's guesses, just encourage them to observe, think, and express their own ideas.

Gift Collecting/Distributing

Value   Christmas

We managed to think of a variety of gifts the children could collect or distribute in unusual ways at this time of year. We suggest that visits to nursing homes, etc., be carefully evaluated. Such facilities often have many visitors at this time of year and are forgotten at other times. Those kinds of trips might be appreciated more by all if they are scheduled later in the winter or spring.

Ideas: Collect wood for the church fireplace if you have someone who will allow you to cut a downed tree on their property.
Set up and maintain a bird feeder.
Take clothing donations to a local distribution center.

Nativity Tour

Value   Christmas
New Life

I have always wanted to take a tour of nativities set up by various churches and other groups to let the children see what a variety of representations there are of this very special event. We have not had many such displays in our vicinity. We have, however, had most enjoyable trips to a local cemetery and mausoleum which have a nativity including live animals and many small and charming Christmas and winter scenes set up by a flower shop. We have learned to look in unusual places for good trips.

With some thought, you can do much better than the usual trip to local shopping centers to see Santa Claus or the decorations. Both of these are fun, and might be very good family activities, but they do not reinforce our goal to experience Christmas in non-commercial ways.

VISITORS

A Carpenter or Woodworker

A Park Ranger or Naturalist
to talk about how animals live in winter

A Ski Resort Operator
to talk about how people enjoy the out-of-doors
in all kinds of weather

FINGER PLAYS ...AND SONGS

Baby Jesus

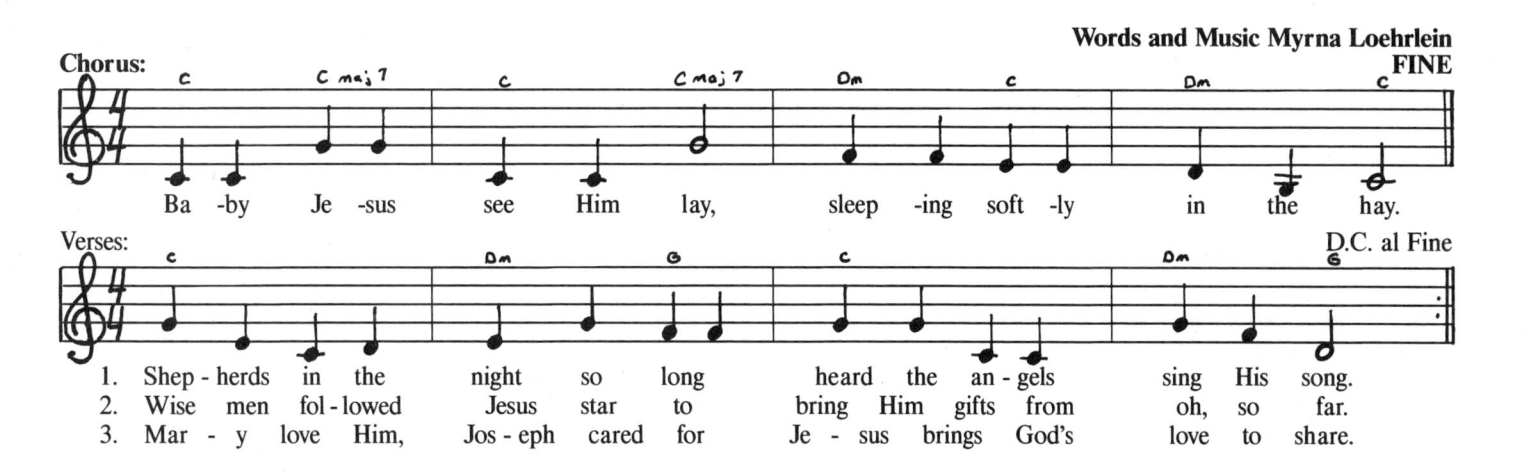

Words and Music Myrna Loehrlein

Chorus:
Ba-by Jesus see Him lay, sleep-ing soft-ly in the hay.

Verses:
1. Shep-herds in the night so long heard the an-gels sing His song.
2. Wise men fol-lowed Jesus star to bring Him gifts from oh, so far.
3. Mar-y love Him, Jos-eph cared for Je-sus brings God's love to share.

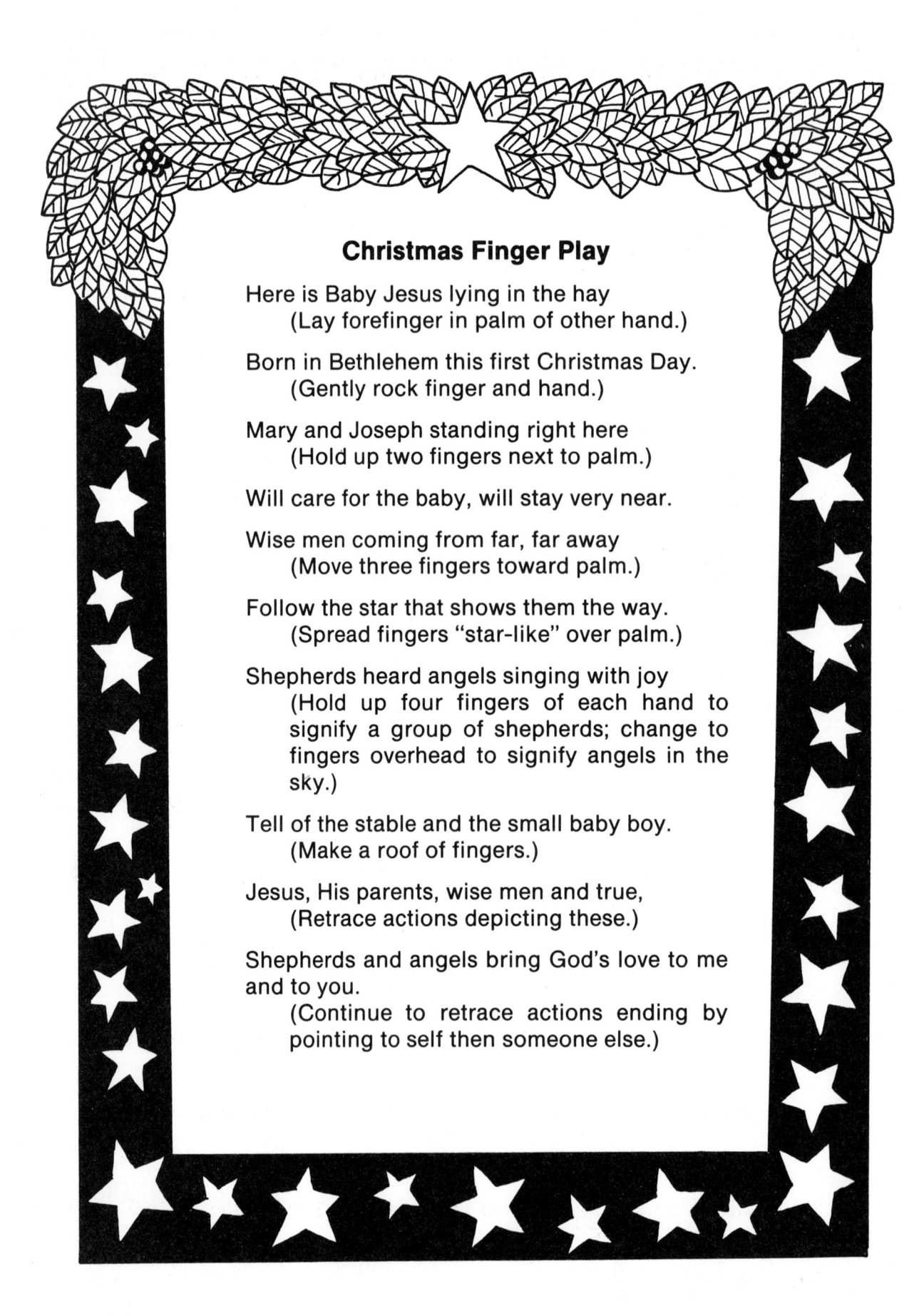

Christmas Finger Play

Here is Baby Jesus lying in the hay
   (Lay forefinger in palm of other hand.)

Born in Bethlehem this first Christmas Day.
   (Gently rock finger and hand.)

Mary and Joseph standing right here
   (Hold up two fingers next to palm.)

Will care for the baby, will stay very near.

Wise men coming from far, far away
   (Move three fingers toward palm.)

Follow the star that shows them the way.
   (Spread fingers "star-like" over palm.)

Shepherds heard angels singing with joy
   (Hold up four fingers of each hand to signify a group of shepherds; change to fingers overhead to signify angels in the sky.)

Tell of the stable and the small baby boy.
   (Make a roof of fingers.)

Jesus, His parents, wise men and true,
   (Retrace actions depicting these.)

Shepherds and angels bring God's love to me and to you.
   (Continue to retrace actions ending by pointing to self then someone else.)

BOOKS AND RESOURCES

Bible Stories

    Jesus' Birth—Matthew 2:1-12, Luke 2:2-28
    Sermon on the Mount (Lillies and Birds)—Matthew 6:25-30
    Feeding the Multitude—Luke 9:10-17

Books

Anglund, Jean W., *Christmas Is a Time of Giving*, Illus., San Diego: Harcourt, Brace, Jovanovich, Inc., 1961.

Davidson, Alice J., *The Story of Baby Moses*, Gibson, 1985.

Lee, Sharon, *Joyous Days: A Collection of Advent and Christmas Activities,* Minneapolis: Winston Press, Inc., 1984.

Mel, Charles L. Jr., *Happy Birthday Baby Jesus*, Ken Munowitz, illus., San Francisco: Harper & Row, 1976.

Mitgutsch, Ali, *From Tree to Table*, Carolrhoda Books, 1981.

Muller, Rolf, *A Very Noisy Day*, Atheneum, 1981.

Neff, Lavonne, *God's Gift Baby, Concordia Press, 1977.*

Peet, Bill, *Cowardly Clyde*, Houghton-Mifflin, 1981.

Piper, Watty, *The Little Engine That Could*, George and Doris Hauman, illus., Scholastic, Inc., 1979.

Robbins, Ruth, *Baboushka and the Three Kings*, Sidjakov Nicholas, illus., Boston: Houghton-Mifflin Co., 1960

Roberts, Jim and Scheck, Joann, *When Jesus was a Boy*, Augsburg, 1978.

Wangerin, W. Jr., *The Baby God Promised*, Concordia Press, 1976.

Warren, Mary P, *On Our Way to Christmas: A Family Activity Book for Advent*, Minneapolis: Augsburg, 1980.

Winthrop, Elizabeth, *Being Brave Is Best*, Tom Cooke, illus., Parker Brothers, 1984.

Records

Millang, Steve and Scelsa, Greg, *We All Live Together,* Vol. 3, "Shapes," 1979, Youngheart Records, Los Angeles, CA 90027.

    —vol. 2, "Number Rock."

Rogers, Fred, *A Place of Our Own*, "I Did Too" (confidence), Family Communications, Inc., 4802 Fifth Ave., Pittsburgh, PA 15213.

COMMUNITY HELPERS/ STEWARDSHIP
February and March

Objectives 59
Crafts
    Name Mobiles 61
    Name Tags 61
    Bags and Briefcases 62
    Happy/Sad Tooth 62
    Safe Touch 63
    Name Flower 64
    Dominoes 64
    Kerchoo! 64
    Mist Paint 65
    Sun Pictures 65
    Ring Toss Target 65
Learning Games
    Career Charades 66
    Post Office 66
    Animal Walks 67
    Stone Soup 67
    Fruit Salad 67
    Safe Touch: "What If?" 68
    Ambulatory Aids 68
    Doing It Differently 68
    Throw! 69
    Bounce and Roll 69
    Catch! 69
Snacks 70
Show-and-Tell
    Community Helpers 71
    Good Health 71
Field Trips
    Work Fun 72
    Health Care 72
    Ecology 72
Visitors 73
Finger Plays . . . and Songs
    Helpers 74
    The Light 74
    Go, Teeth, Go! 74
Books and Resources 75

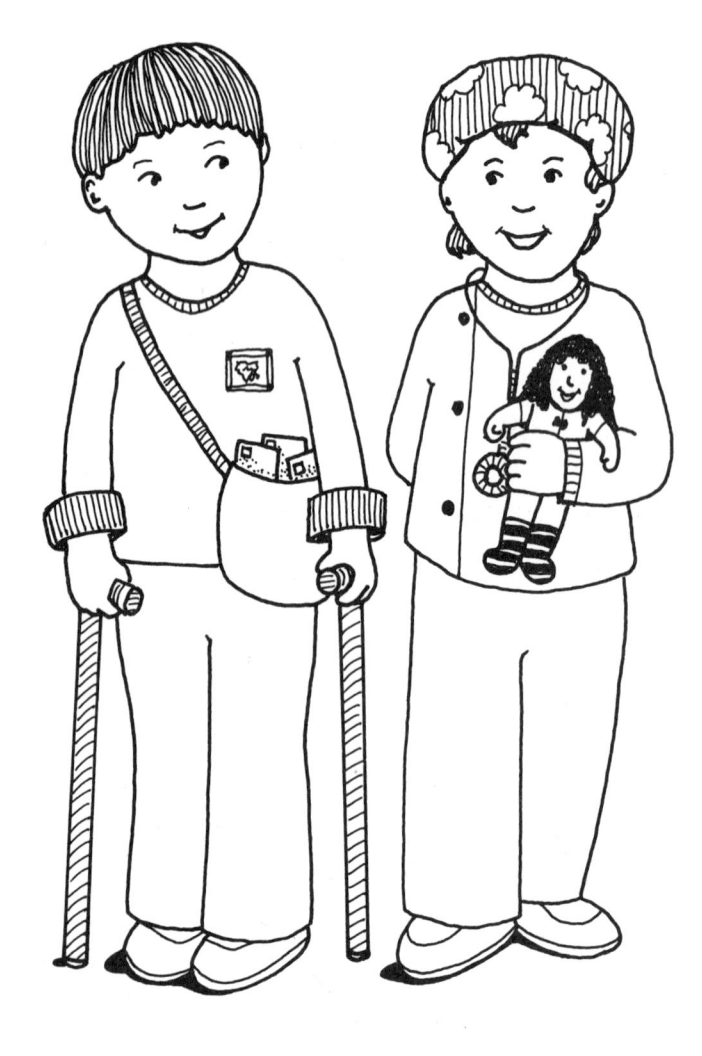

Objectives for Community Helpers/Stewardship Unit

VALUE OBJECTIVES

1. To take responsiblity for use of time, talents, energy

2. To be aware of our interdependence

3. To know that work can be fun

4. To take more responsibility for health and hygiene

5. To accept others who are different or handicapped

6. To gain and practice developmental skills

SKILL OBJECTIVES (3 to 4-year-olds)

A. To gain skill in conflict resolution

B. To recognize first name in print and print first letter

C. To recognize and name the numerals from 1 to 5

D. To gain skill in pencil/crayon grip

E. To gain skill in throwing and catching

F. To recognize and name the colors red (February) and purple (March)

G. To practice cutting in a straight line

H. To practice formerly introduced skills

SURVIVAL SKILL

I. To use "Safe Touch" skills

SKILL OBJECTIVES (5 to 6-year-olds)

    A. To gain skill in conflict resolution

    B. To recognize own name and print it using lower case letters

    C. To recognize and name numerals 1-10

    D. To practice pencil/crayon grip

    E. To gain skill in throwing and catching

    F. To practice cutting straight and curved lines

    G. To practice formerly introduced skills

SURVIVAL SKILL

    H. To know and use "Safe Touch" skills

CRAFTS

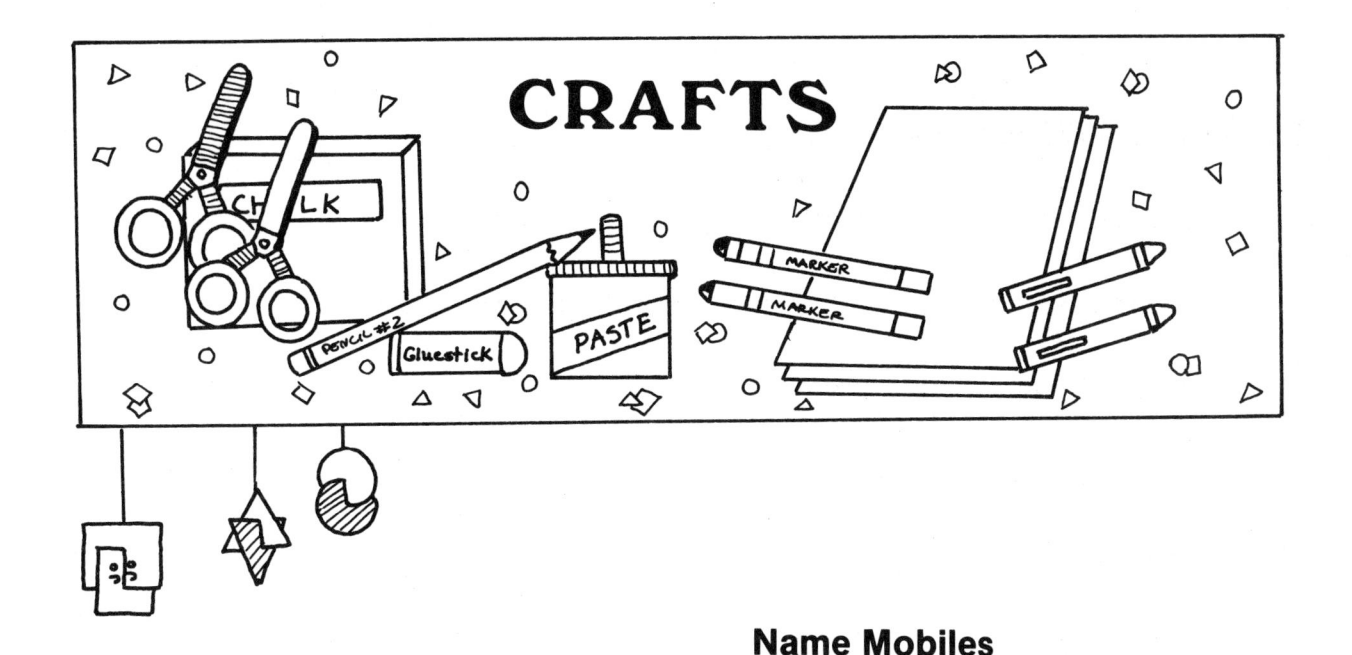

Name Mobiles

Concept   Skill Development

Skill   Name
Shapes
Grip
Scissors

Child traces and/or cuts two matching shapes from colored paper. Cut slits halfway down from the top of one and halfway up from the bottom of the other. Child writes his/her name on each side of each center giving eight chances to practice writing his/her name (or as many as each child can handle). Slip the shapes together and hang from ceiling.

Name Tags

Concept   Skill Development

Skill   Name
Grip
Scissors

Children can create name tags to be worn at preschool. (We do not recommend self-made name tags for field trips when clear identification is important.) Provide an assortment of paper, bits of lace and other scraps, stickers, markers, etc. Names should be clearly and carefully written. Otherwise, let the imagination of the creator lead the way.

Bags and Briefcases

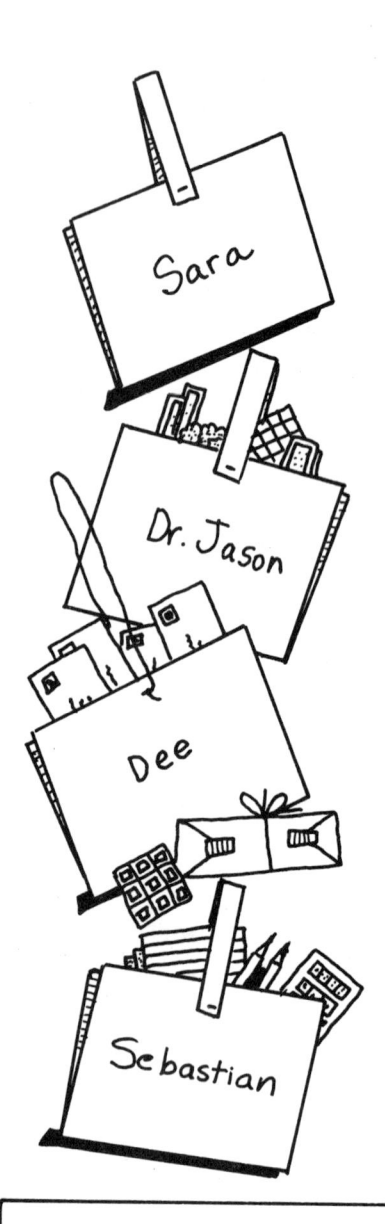

Concept　　Workfun

Skill　　Grip
　　　　　　Name
　　　　　　Numerals

Make medical bags, postal bags, and briefcases as follows:

Cut a 1" strip from a manilla file folder. Staple it to either side of the top of a whole folder to form a handle. Child writes his/her name on both sides of the bag/briefcase then fills it with appropriate equipment.

Medical bag: Band-Aids, a cotton ball, motel soap bars, gauze or clean cotton fabric scraps.

Postal bag: Replace the 1" strip handle with a piece of yarn long enough to go over the child's shoulder. Fill the bag with junk mail, envelopes child has addressed perhaps with invented writing, stamps (stickers from record or magazine direct mail promotions work well), small boxes to serve as packages to deliver (bank check boxes serve well for this).

Briefcase: lined paper or a few sheets from a yellow lined pad, a pencil, an eraser, an oaktag or cardboard calculator.

Happy/Sad Tooth

Concept　　Good Health

Skill　　Grip/Classify

Child cuts a small meat tray in half. Mount each half, cut side up, on one side of a firm mounting board creased in the center so it stands on a table. (Tacky glue works best for gluing form.) Child draws a happy-faced tooth and a sad-faced tooth and glues one to each pocket. Child can sort food pictures putting healthful foods into the happy tooth pocket and less healthful foods into the sad tooth pocket.

Safe Touch

Concept   Good Health

Skill   Safe Touch

Child simply draws or paints a picture of himself/herself. The picture is attached to a letter asking parents to discuss with the child the principles of safe touch:

> ownership of their own bodies
> private places on their bodies
> correct names for anatomical parts
> the importance of telling someone they trust of unsafe touches or attempts
> the importance of saying "NO" with assurance, how and when to do it

More specific information can usually be obtained from your local hospital.

Name Flower

Concept Skill Development

Skill Grip
Name

Teacher provides various colors of construction paper with a simple flower stem drawn on. Child writes name to form petals and may add details like sun, clouds, insects, animals, people, etc.

Dominoes

Concept Skill Development

Skill Numerals
Grip
Paste/Glue

Provide 5 to 10 thick cardboard pieces about 2" × 4". Mat board scraps obtained from picture framing stores work well. Child puts a set of small paste-ons (reinforcement rings work well for numbers up to 5), on one half of a domino and a different numeral on the other half. Child then lines up his dominoes to match the set to its representative numeral.

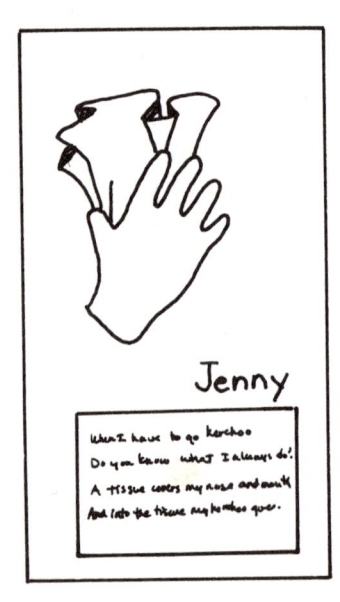

Kerchoo!

Concept Good Health
Ecology

Skill Grip
Glue/Paste
Scissors

Child traces around his/her hand and cuts it out. Younger children will need help. On a mounting board, a paper plate, large mat board scrap, or other paper, child glues a facial tissue with the cut out hand over it as if holding it. Somewhere on the mounting board, add this little rhyme:

> When I have to go kerchoo
> Do you know what I always do?
> A tissue covers my mouth and nose,
> And into the tissue my kerchoo goes.

Mist Paint

Concept Ecology
Skill Name
Numerals

Child uses rings of tape or double-faced tape to secure onto large paper cutouts of the letters in his/her name or of numerals being studied. Child then sprinkles one or two colors of dry tempera over all. Child's paper is set out in a light rain or child may make it "rain" using a spray bottle. Paper should be evenly well dampened but not soaked.

Sun Pictures

Concept Ecology
Skill Name
Numerals

Similar to mist painting above except the cutouts are secured to blueprint paper and set in the sun to achieve design. These two crafts are especially effective when done as a set in a study of weather.

Ring Toss Target

Concept Skill Development
Skill Ball Skills

Split one end of a paper towel tube with 4 to 6, 1" splits to form tabs. Open the tabs to glue them onto a square cut from corregated cardboard or other sturdy material. Child may decorate target with paint, Con-Tact paper scraps, or glue-on paper scraps. Plastic container lids with the middle cut out make good rings to toss over this target.

LEARNING GAMES

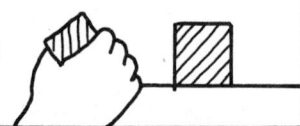

Career Charades

Concept Time/Talent

Skill Observation

Child pantomimes a job while group tries to guess it. Child may choose parent's job, own expected job when grown, or jobs done to help around the house.

Post Office

Concept Workfun
Time/Talents

Skill Name
Classify

Make post office boxes from cardboard boxes with dividers by turning them on their sides. Using pastel colored envelopes, mark at least one envelope for each child with his/her name and a sticker or other individual symbol. Mark each box with a similarly colored tag showing the child's name and sticker or other symbol. Mark one small box with each envelope color. The children may then sort the mail by matching names, symbols, or simple colors.

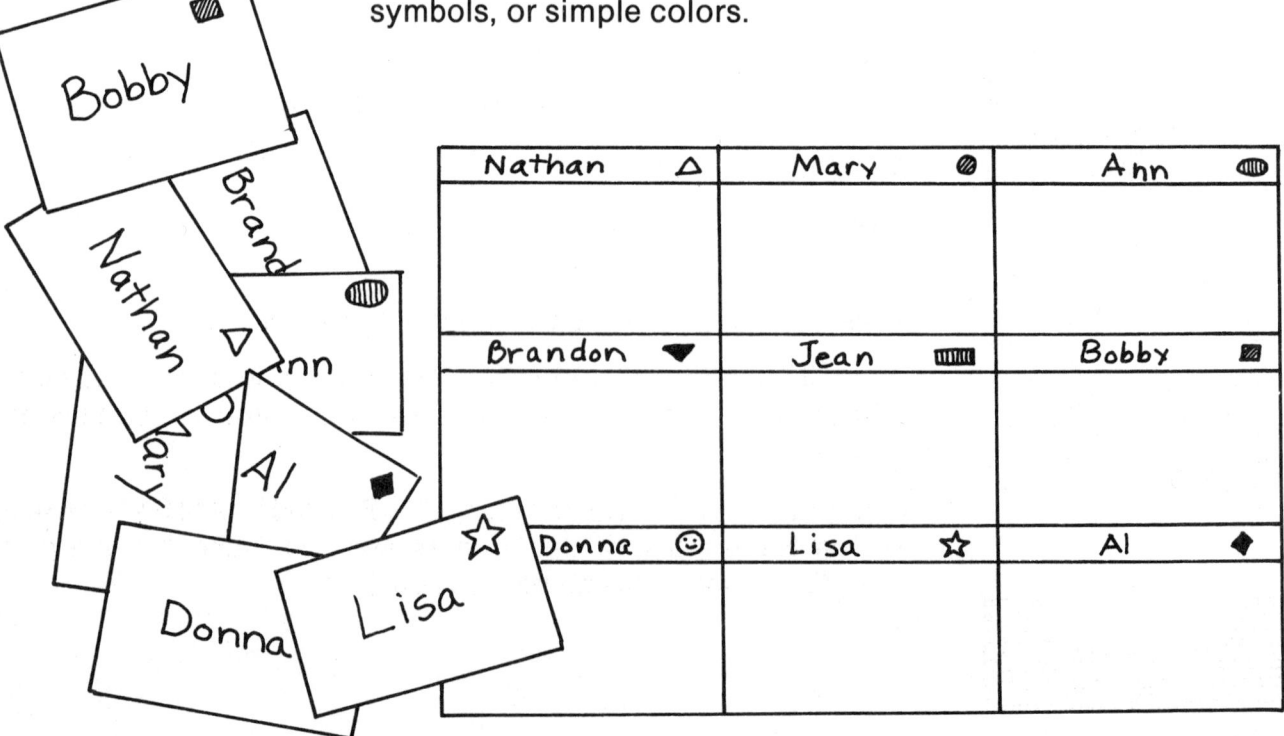

Animal Walks

Concept Ecology

Skill Muscle Skills
Observation

Child walks around the circle imitating an animal. Children guess the animal being imitated.

Stone Soup

Concept Good Health

Skill Classify
Muscle Skills

Read the story "Stone Soup" (see page 75). Review items the citizens added to the soup. Children are invited to bring something to add to their soup. Before making the soup, class may classify contributions by general food group, color, texture, size of container, or other factors children might suggest. Children then assist in cleaning and chopping vegetables and stirring the soup. They may even pack up small quantities to take home to give their families a taste.

Note: If you do not have available stones or rocks which you trust in a soup pot, we have used a rutabaga. It looks like rock and makes the soup taste great.

Fruit Salad

Concept Good Health

Skill Classify
Muscle Skills

This is similar to Stone Soup, but no story is used.

Note: This unit is a good time to include preparation of plenty of nutritious snacks, based on fresh fruits and vegetables and whole grains.

The story of the "Little Red Hen," "THE GIANT JAM SANDWICH" or the Bible story of the "Loaves and the Fishes" make good associations with bread baking activities.

Safe Touch: "What If?"

Concept   Good Health

Skill   Safe Touch

After discussing the principles of "safe touch" let the children practice role playing ways in which they would handle a safe touch problem. Be sure to give them plenty of practice at saying "no" assertively, telling someone they trust about the incident, knowing that such incidents are not their fault, and knowing that their friends and families will still love them if such a thing should happen to them and they tell about it.

Ambulatory Aids

Concept   Good Health
Time/Talent
Acceptance
Workfun

Skill   Muscle Skills
Observation

Invite a physical therapist, occupational therapist, or other medical professional or talk to one yourself to find out what you can about wheel chairs, crutches, walkers. Bring these items to preschool to talk about and let the children try them out. Follow up this activity with a trip to a nursing home, perhaps to distribute valentines.

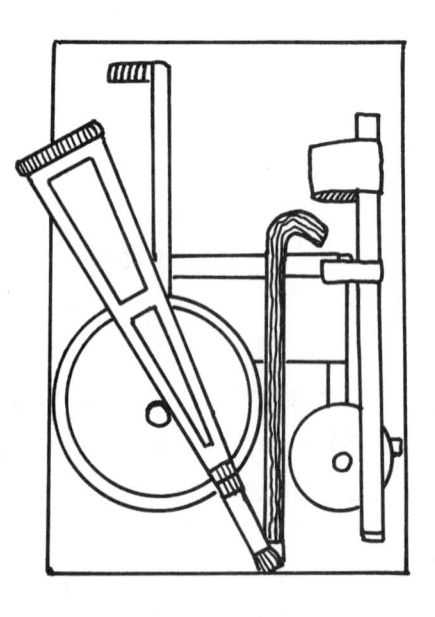

Doing It Differently

Concept   Acceptance
Good Health

Skill   Muscle Skills
Observation

Children discuss the adjustments that would be necessitated by various handicapping conditions. They may guess how it would feel, what would have to be done differently, ways in which other people could help or cause additional problems. After some thought, the children may spend a short time playing, eating snack, etc., as if they have a given handicapping condition.

Throw!

Concept Skill Development

Skill Ball Skills

Start with beanbags, as they are easier to control, and throw.

to a partner	into: buckets
as high as possible	baskets
as far as possible	targets
while standing on two feet	hard
while standing on one foot	gentle
kneeling	using a container
sitting	as if: angry
with either hand	sleepy
very quickly	scared
very slowly	silly

Give opportunities to throw every day if possible. Try to include less athletic children in a successful experience.

Bounce and Roll

Concept Skill Development

Skill Ball Skills

Bounce and roll a ball in as many configurations and situations as you can think of:

ROLL	BOUNCE
to a partner	to a partner
to a target	to a target
to bounce off a wall	as high as possible
while sitting	while sitting
while standing	while standing
hard	bounce and catch
gently	bounce several times
with an instrument	with an instrument
(broom, paddle, etc.)	(paddle, on a string)

Catch!

Concept Skill Development

Skill Ball Skills

Catch a beanbag or ball in as many ways and situations as you can invent.

a big ball	one thrown: high	with: feet	when just a little
a small ball	level	hands	surprised
in a container	fast	while: sitting	being rolled
with a glove	slow	expecting it	

Shining Star Publications, Copyright © 1990, A division of Good Apple, Inc.   SS1875

SNACKS

Some snacks are suggested in the "Crafts" section.

Red Snacks:	Purple Snacks:
cranberry juice	purple grapes
cranberry sauce	grape juice
radishes and dip	eggplant and dip
cherry tomatoes	red cabbage slaw
frozen berries	grape juice bars

Any fresh fruit or fresh vegetable snacks

Fruits canned without sugar

Fruit and/or vegetable juices

Whole grain breads

Whole grain cereals

Vegetable soups or salads

Fruit soups or salads

SHOW-AND-TELL

Community Helpers

Tools of the trade, objects used by Mom or Dad in their work

Memento of a community helper service:

mail
a light bulb
token from a service station
wrapped hanger from dry cleaner
brochure from lawn service
garbage bags
a newspaper

Good Health

Tooth care:

toothbrush
toothpaste
dental floss
baby tooth
healthful food
dental instrument
token or "prize" from a dental visit

Health, fitness and safety:

demonstrate a healthful exercise
fitness equipment
a brochure about fitness business or technqiue
vitamins
book about fitness or safety
cabinet door lock
electric outlet safety plug
prosthetic device

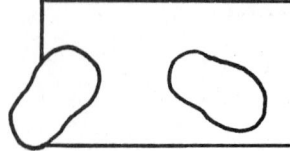

FIELD TRIPS

Work Fun

Almost any community business or service institution will make a good trip for this unit. If you visit common places like the supermarket or local bakery, be sure to show the children the parts they don't usually see.

Some suggestions:
- bakery
- supermarket
- pediatrician
- toy factory or toy store
- fast food restaurant
- theater where live performances are presented

A special treat comes if you can visit the workplace of a parent.

Health Care

Try to think of health care in its broadest terms.

Some suggestions:
- hospital
- dentist
- pediatrician
- a maker of prosthesis
- health or exercise center
- health food store
- exercise track

Again, a visit to a parent's workplace is almost always a first choice.

Ecology

This concept is about our interdependence, not just the balance of nature, although you may find that nature is a good place to start.

Some suggestions:
- nursing home
- fire station
- courtroom
- sanitation dept.
- nature center or woods or park
- fish hatchery
- garden center

VISITORS

Concept Workfun
Time/Talent

This is the time to invite parents to share their occupations with the children. Have come as many parents as can, and as you can reasonably fit into your program. We have had an airline pilot, doctors, homemakers, school janitors, etc.

Concept Good Health

Nurse or nutritionist or dietician to talk about healthful eating

School or visiting nurse

Firefighter or police officer to talk about safety

Concept Acceptance

Someone with a handicapping condition to explain how they get along by doing some things differently

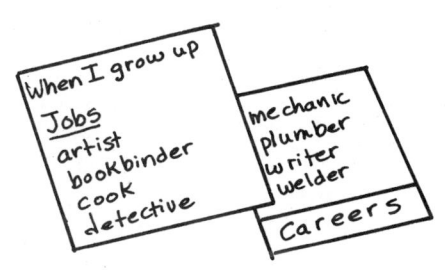

Concept Time/Talents

A career counselor

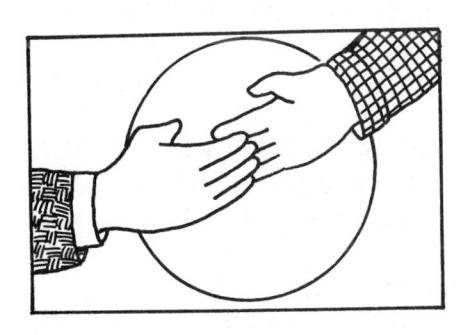

Skill Conflict

Someone who deals with conflict resolution or negotiations

A mental health professional or paraprofessional

Skill Name

Someone who engraves or personalizes gifts

FINGER PLAYS ...AND SONGS

Helpers

I can help at my house
You can help at yours.

Lots of friendly people
Help us in the stores.

Crossing guards can help us
Get across the street.

Waitresses can help us
When we need a treat.

Doctors, nurses, dentists
Help us grow up strong.

Teachers help us learn things
As we go along.

Moms, Dads, Grandpas, and Grandmas
Show us what to do.

Best of all, God helps me
And God gives help to you.

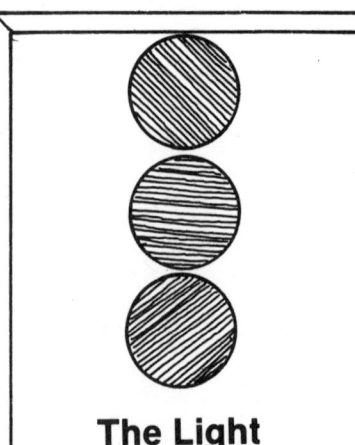

Go, Teeth, Go!

(To be chanted as if it were a football cheer!)

Scrub a tooth!
Scrub a tooth!
Get it really clean.
Scrub a tooth!
Scrub a tooth!
Make it really gleam.

Munch a veggie
Munch a fruit
Give your teeth a treat.
Munch a cracker
Cer-e-al
Made of good whole wheat!

See your dentist
See him soon,
Two times every year.
Give your teeth your very best
And give yourself a cheer!

The Light

Red means stop
Green means go
Yellow means wait
Even if you're late.

BOOKS AND RESOURCES

Bible Stories
    Good Samaritan—Luke 10:30-37
    Talents—Matthew 25:14-30

Books

Community Helpers

Adams, Phyllis,. *Pippin Goes to Work*, Cleveland, OH: Modern Curriculum Pess, 1983.

Harwood, Pearl A., *Mr. Bumba's New Job*, Joseph Folger, illus., Minneapolis, MN: Lerner Publications, 1964.

Lasher, Joe, *Mothers Can Do Anything*, Chicago, Albert Whitman Co., 1976.

Scarry, Richard, *What Do People Do All Day?* New York: Random, 1968.

Ecology

DePaola, Tomie, *Michael Bird Boy*, Treehouse, 1975.

Givens, Janet E., *Something Wonderful Happened*, Susan Dodge, illus., New York: Atheneum, 1982.

Rothman, Joel, *Once There Was a Stream*, Bruce Roberts, photos, Merrick, NY: Scroll Press, 1973.

Health

Berenstain, Stan and Janice, *The Berenstain Bears and the Messy Room*, New York: Random, 1983.

Vigna, Judith, *The Little Boy Who Loved Dirt and Almost Became a Superslob*, A. Witman, 1975.

Safety

Beal, Randy, *Never Take Candy from a Stranger*, Memphis, TN: R.B. Publications, 1984.

Berry, Joy, *Teach Me About Danger*, Chris Sharp, illus., Newark, NJ: Peter Pan, 1984.

Nutrition

Berry, Joy, *Teach Me About Mealtime*, Kelly Orly, ed., Chris Sharp, illus., Newark, NJ: Peter Pan, 1984.

Brown, Marica, *Stone Soup*, New York: Charles Scribner's Sons, 1947.

Moncure, Jane, *The Healthkin Food Train*, Helen Endres, illus., Elgin, IL: Child's World, 1982.

Rhodes, Janis, *Nutrition Mission*, Carthage, IL: Good Apple, Inc., 1982.

Acceptance

Kohler, Christine, *I Help the Handicapped*, 1985.

Lionni, Leo, *Swimmy*, New York: Pantheon, 1968.

Conflict

Crary, Elizabeth, *I Want It*, Marina Magale, illus., Seattle, WA: Parenting Press, 1982.

_____ *I Want to Play*, Marina Magale, illus., Seattle, WA: Parenting Press, 1982.

_____ *My Name is Not Dummy*, Marina Magale, illus., Seattle, WA: Parenting Press, 1982.

_____ *I Can't Wait*, Marina Magale, illus., Seattle, WA: Parenting Press, 1982.

Records

Alsop, Peter, *Wha' D' Ya Wanna Do?* "Sandwiches," "Wha 'da 'ya Wanna Do?" Flying Fish Records, 1304 W. Schubert, Chicago, IL 60614.

Millang, Steve and Scelsa, Greg, *We All Live Together* Vol. 2, "Number Rock," 2978, Youngheart Music Education Service, Los Angeles, CA.

Palmer, Hap. *Getting to Know Myself*, "What Do People Do?" Educational Activities, Inc., Freeport, N.Y. 11520.

_____ *Learning Basic Skills Through Music*, "The Elephant," "The Number March," "This is the Way We Get Up in the Morning," "What Are You Wearing?" "What Is Your Name?" Educational Activities, Inc., Freeport, N.Y. 11520.

GROWING THINGS
April and May

Objectives 78
Crafts
   Butterfly Sequence 80
   Caterpillar on a Twig 80
   Tissue Paper Texture 81
   Seed Collage.....................81
   Dough Nests 81
Learning Games
   Jump Course.....................82
   Role Playing: Lost 82
Snacks 83
Field Trips 84
Show-and-Tell 86
Finger Plays . . . and Songs
   Willie 87
   Growing 87
Books and Resources..............88

Objectives for Growing Things Unit

VALUE OBJECTIVES

1. To become aware of God's gift of eternal life as seen in Spring

2. To see that all people grow and change

3. To understand that change is a part of life

4. To see Easter as the celebration of God's gift of eternal and renewing life

5. To gain and practice developmental skills

SKILL OBJECTIVES (3 to 4-year-olds)

A. Jumping, hopping

B. To begin to gain a sense of rhythm

C. To recognize and name the letters in own name

D. To sequence 2 or 3 events in a story

E. To practice pasting and gluing

F. To practice formerly introduced skills

SURVIVAL SKILL

G. To avoid hazardous substances

SKILL OBJECTIVES (5 to 6-year-olds)

A. To gain proficiency in hopping, jumping, and possibly, skipping

B. To practice rhythm through music and movement

C. To recognize and name the letters of the alphabet out of sequence

D. To sequence 4 to 6 events in a story

E. To practice cutting curved lines and pencil grip

F. To practice formerly introduced skills

SURVIVAL SKILL

G. To learn what to do if lost in a store or other public place

CRAFTS

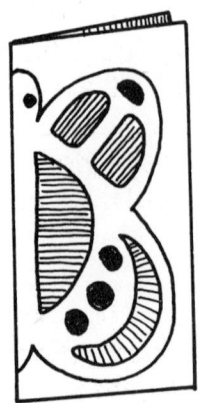

Butterfly Sequence

Concept   Grow and Change

Skill   Paste/Glue
Sequence

Fold a piece of 9" × 12" light-colored paper along its length and cut out a gently rounded butterfly shape. The child colors the butterfly wings and body.

With paper folded, draw or paste on leaves on both outside surfaces. Onto one outside surface, glue a piece of thick yarn to represent a caterpillar. Onto the other side, glue a cotton ball to represent a cocoon. The paper may be folded and opened to reveal the stages and sequence of a butterfly's life cycle.

Caterpillar on a Twig

Concept   Trust Change

Skill   Paste/Glue
Sequence

The sequence of a butterfly's life cycle can be shown on a twig. Near the thicker end of the twig, glue a piece of heavy yarn to represent a caterpillar. Near the middle of the twig, glue a cotton ball to represent a cocoon. Near the tip of the twig, glue a butterfly which the child has colored and cut out.

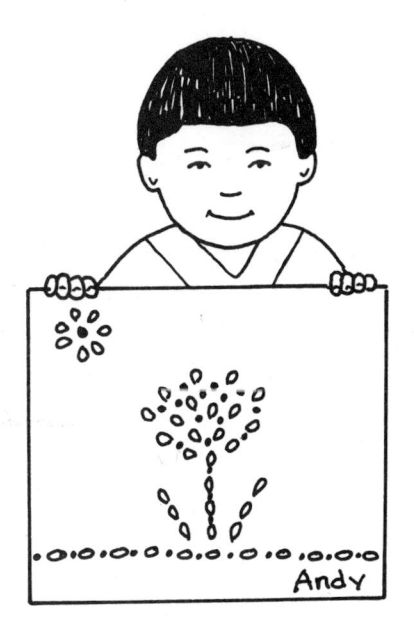

Tissue Paper Texture

Concept   Renewal
             Easter

Skill   Paste/Glue
             Muscle Skills
             Skill Development

This is an effective technique with a variety of applications limited only by your imagination. The basic technique: bunch a 1" square of crepe paper around the blunt end of a pencil. Touch the end into a pool of white glue. Touch the glued paper onto your background paper. Gently lift the pencil out. The crepe paper remains upright and when dry is securely glued into place.

Variation I: Use tissue paper instead of crepe paper.

Variation II: Bunching the paper around the end of the pencil requires considerable fine motor coordination. Less coordinated or younger children may simply crumple the 1" square tightly and glue it on the background.

Seed Collage

Concept   Renewal

Skill   Paste/Glue

You probably made a seed collage in the fall when you talked about plants producing seeds. This is a good time to make another one with seeds of flowers or vegetables that the children can then plant. Flowers producing relatively large seeds are: sunflower, hollyhocks, four o'clocks.

Dough Nests

Concept   Renewal

Skill   Muscle Skills
              Observation

Examine examples of birds' nests, either actual nests or pictures of them. Guide children to discover some of the materials used to build the nests. Take a walk to gather some of these materials—grass, string, leaf, lint, etc. Teacher may provide these materials if a walk is impossible. Children make nests out of Play-Doh and press these materials into their dough nests to represent birds' nests.

LEARNING GAMES

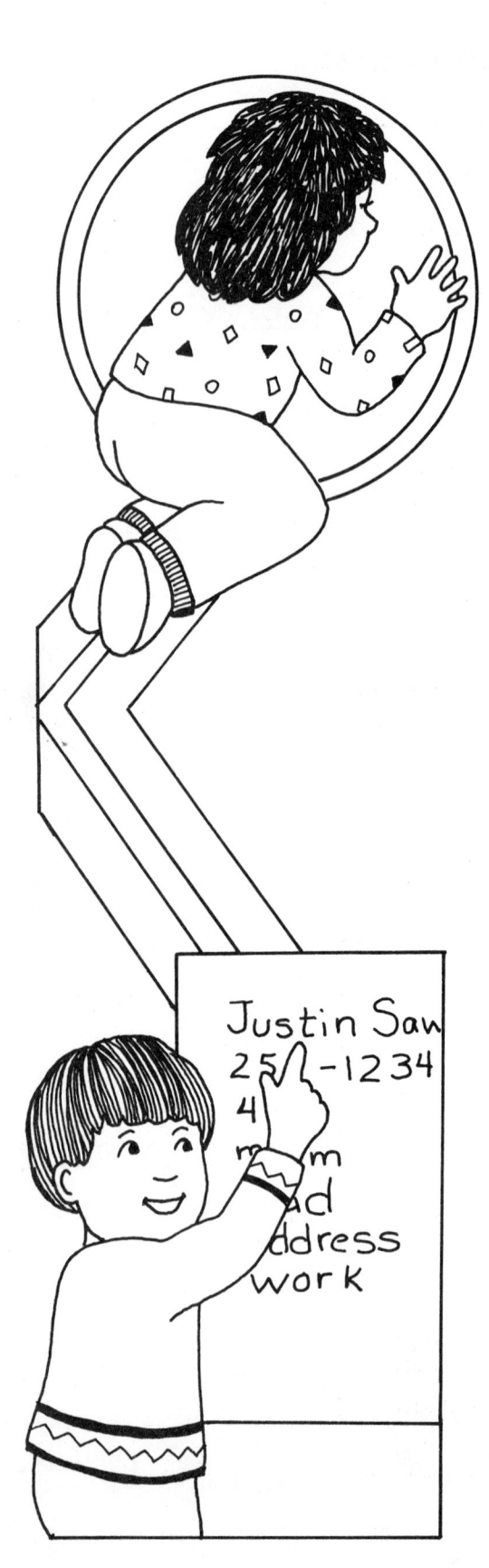

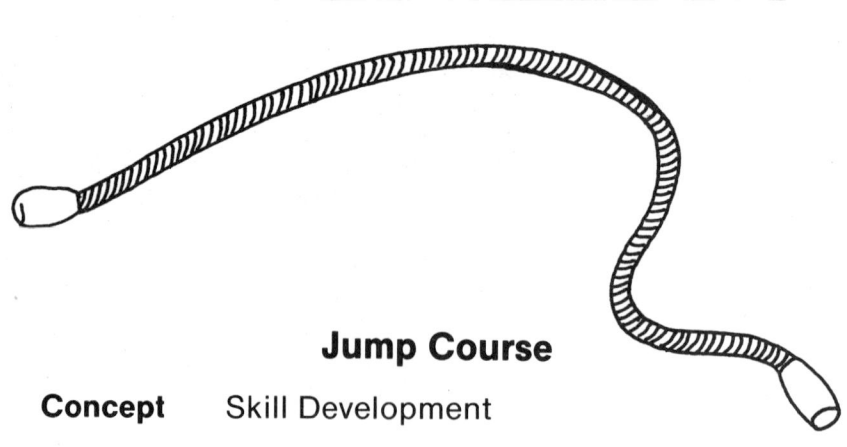

Jump Course

Concept   Skill Development

Skills   Hop/Jump
Hop/Jump/Skip

Build an obstacle course including many things to jump over, into, and off of. You might include: hoops, tires, low barriers or ropes to jump over, low boxes to jump off of, tape or chalk-drawn squares to hop in.

Role Playing: Lost

Concept   Skill Development

Skill   Lost in Public

Children need to be aware of their options should they become lost in public. After discussion of what could happen and hearing some experiences the children or friends may have had, guide the children to begin examining what is to be done should they become lost in a variety of situations. This is a good time for use of puppets, flannelgraph figures, direct role playing, group story writing, etc., to give the children practice in handling being separated from parents or other caregivers in a public place.

Consider with the children being lost: at a large and/or small store, a park, a carnival or festival, in a theater, on a bus, in a shopping mall, on the sidewalk. Discuss and role play who to ask for help, what to tell the helper, what NOT to do when lost. This is an excellent time to review survival information:

child's full name   parents' names
phone   address
age   parents' workplaces

SNACKS

Green Snacks

green eggs and ham
(add a few drops of green food coloring to scrambled eggs.)

green salad

celery

green bean salad

avocado

guacamole

green apples

Yellow Snacks

golden apples

pineapple

cheese

orange juice

summer squash

macaroni and cheese

eggs—hard cooked

Other Snacks:

Growing things—cut open any fresh fruit to find the seeds, then eat the fruit.
Pick, clean, and eat anything growing in your garden.

FIELD TRIPS

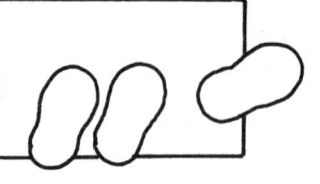

Concept   Growth and Change

Visit a farm to see baby animals and preparations for spring planting.

Concept   Growth and Change

Visit a greenhouse to see plants in various stages of growth.

Concept   Skill Development

Skill   Rhythm

Visit a fitness center or gym to participate in a class or use equipment to practice muscle skills developed throughout the year.

Visit a park or fields nearby to look for signs of spring.

Concept   Trust Change

Visit a nursing home. If you have not visited a nursing home yet, this would be a good time to let children see how people change while they stay interesting, important people.

Concept   Growth and Change

Invite a farmer or farm wife to tell about the care given to baby animals and the ways in which they grow and change.

Concept   Growth and Change

Invite an animal breeder to tell about how he cares for his mothers and young animals.

Concept   Trust Change

Invite an elderly person to tell about life when he/she was a child. If they could bring some toys, tools, or other objects of their childhood that the children could handle, it would be even more effective.

SHOW-AND-TELL

Concept   Growth and Change

A baby or young pet

Concept   Renewal

Seed packets or seeds or seedlings for spring planting

Concept   Trust Change

A baby or parent or grandparent from the child's family This is especially appropriate if the adult visitors bring pictures from their childhood.

Concept   Renewal

Spring flowers or other signs of spring

Concept   Trust Change

Mementos from kindergarten round-up or a visit to the school where the child will attend kindergarten.

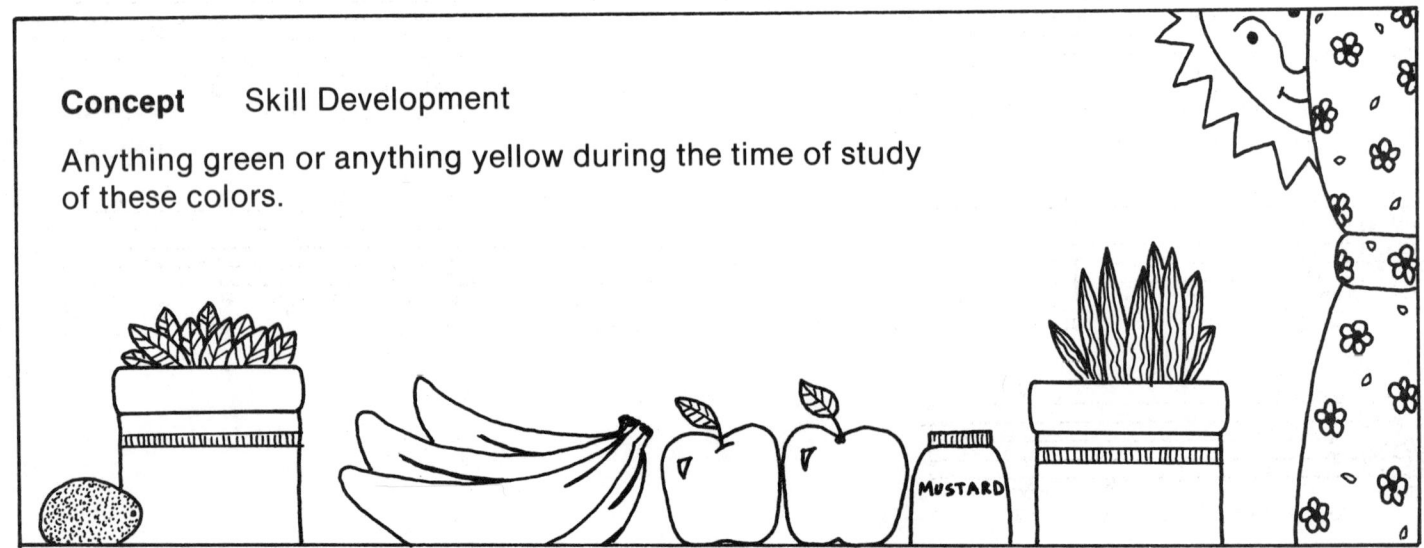

Concept   Skill Development

Anything green or anything yellow during the time of study of these colors.

FINGER PLAYS ...AND SONGS

Growing

Once a little baby lay
Here in her crib so cozy.
She played with her fingers
And sucked her thumb
And tickled her little toes-y.
But soon she grew both tall and strong
Now she's a big girl you see
Because God made that little girl
To grow up to be me!

Willie

(Words and Music by Myrna Loehrlein)

1. Willie was a caterpillar long and fat and brown. Willie was a caterpillar crawling on the ground. One day very soon He made a small cocoon Butterfly! (spoken)

2. Willie was a caterpillar wished that he could fly. Willie was a caterpillar longed to touch the sky.

3. Willie was a butterfly Oh what a big surprise. Willie was a butterfly. His colors filled the sky.

87

BOOKS AND RESOURCES

Bible Stories
  Jesus Cares About Children—Matthew 19:14
  Heals Jarius' Daughter—Matthew 9:18,19,23-26
  Calls the Children to Him—Matthew 18:1-15

Books

Growing

Bruna, Dick, *When I'm Big*, Price Stern, 1984.

Eastman, P.D., *Flap Your Wings*, New York: Random House, 1985.

Krauss, Ruth, *Growing Story*, Phyllis Rowand, illus., New York: 1945.

Spring

Allington, Richard L. and Krull, Kathleen, *Spring*, Dee Rahn, illus., Milwaukee, WI: Raintree Publications, Inc., 1981.

Anglund, Joan W., *Spring Is a New Beginning*, San Diego, CA: Harcourt, Brace, Jovanovich, Inc., 1963.

Karuss, Ruth, *The Carrot Seed*, Crockett Johnson, illus., New York: Harper & Row Junior Books, 1945.

Moncure, Jane B., *Spring Is Here!* Chicago, IL: Children's Press, 1975.

Easter

Grune, Carol, *Kiri and the First Easter*, St. Louis, MO: Concordia Publishing House, 1972.

Wiersum, Beverly, *The Story of Easter for Children*, Lorraine Wells, illus., Ideals, 1979.

Lost

Crary, Elizabeth, *I'm Lost*, Marina Megale, illus., Seattle, WA: Parenting Press, 1985.

Records

Millang, Steve and Scelsa, Greg, *We All Live Together*, Vol. 2, "The Freeze", 1978, Youngheart Music Education Service, Los Angeles, CA

Palmer, Hap, *Getting to Know Myself*, "Sammy," Educational Activities, Inc., Freeport, NY

_____ *Learning Basic Skills Through Music*, Vol. 1, "Growing."

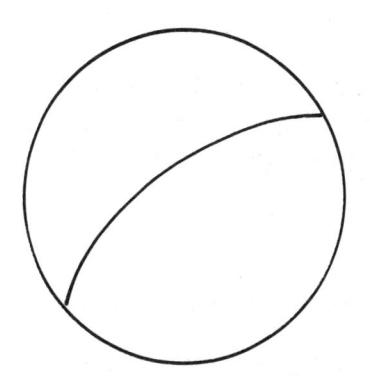

JOY AND CELEBRATION
June and July

Objectives 90
Crafts
   Crepe Paper Streamers 90
   Tissue Paint......................90
Snacks 91
Field Trips 91
Spring Cleaning 92
Show-and-Tell 93
Visitors 93
Books and Resources................94
Awards 95

Shining Star Publications, Copyright © 1990, A division of Good Apple, Inc.

Objectives for Joy and Celebration Unit

VALUE OBJECTIVES

1. To recognize that activities and experiences come to a close

2. To celebrate the growth of children and adults alike in this year together

3. To gain and practice developmental skills

SURVIVAL SKILL (3 to 4-year-olds)

   A. To use seat belts whenever you are in a car

SURVIVAL SKILL (5 to 6-year-olds)

   A. To know and use summer safety skills

CRAFTS

Crepe Paper Streamers

Concept   Celebration

Fold a lightweight paper plate in half. Have an assortment of crepe paper streamers (3'-4' long) available for the children to choose from. Children choose 3-5 streamers to glue onto their plate leaving one half of the ring free of streamers so that it can be used as a handle. Children will enjoy running to make the streamers flow out behind.

Tissue Paint

Concept   Celebration

Did you know you can paint with tissue paper? Just wet it and paint! The color comes right out of the paper.

SNACKS

Make your own ice cream

Place ice cream mix in a one-pound coffee can. Cover tightly and set it inside a three-pound coffee can. Surround the one-pound can with ice, a little water and salt, and put the lid on the three-pound can. The children can then roll the assembly back and forth until the ice cream is frozen. It usually takes about 20-30 minutes. This ice cream will be very cold and will melt quickly (there is not much air in it) and you will have to replace the ice and brine once or twice. It is very good and the children will have great fun making it.

Fruitshakes

This idea is good anytime you need a quick snack from stored supplies and you cannot stand the idea of another snack of crackers.

Into a blender bowl, place 1 cup of dry milk powder. Add fruit of any kind, fresh or canned (well drained). To make it creamier, you may add one tablespoon of dry, non-dairy coffee creamer. This is a satisfying snack, has great variety, and is festive if you add a drinking straw to each glass.

FIELD TRIPS

A family picnic
A trip to a park on a city bus

SPRING CLEANING

Concept   Conclusion

This is a good time to clean up and put away. Let the children plan the order of the work and do as much as they can. They can help take down bulletin boards and other room decorations to be removed for storage. They can wash many of the toys and pack them in boxes or cabinets. They can even wash windows, vacuum, dust, etc., though you will probably have to do these things over again. This activity is not to get the room clean so much as it is to let the children participate in a time of conclusion for the year.

SHOW-AND-TELL

Something used only in the summer
   swimsuits
   beach pails and buckets
   suntan lotion
   sun hats

Tokens of summer activities
   pictures of last year's summer vacation
   summer toys—including bicycles, of course!
   maps or brochures about summer travels

VISITORS

You may not even have any visitors for this unit since it is so short, but if you do, we suggest these:

A crossing guard—to talk about safe ways to cross streets in the summer or on the way to school

A life guard—to talk about water safety

Someone from Parks and Recreation—to talk about summer programs and park safety

Someone from the library—to talk about the summer reading program

BOOKS AND RESOURCES

Bible Stories
    Celebration of Jesus' Entry into Jerusalem—Matthew 21:1-9

Books

Ahlberg, Janet and Ahlberg, Allan, *Playmates*, New York: Viking, 1985.

Cooke, Tom, *Sesame Street Playtime Book*, New York: Random House, 1982.

Let's Play, New York, Putnam Publishing Group, 1978.

Moncure, Jane B, *Summer Is Here!* Chicago, IL: Children's Press, 1975.

Parish, Peggy, *I Can—Can You* (series), New York: Greenwillow, 1984.

Play Safe, Golden Books, Western Publishing, 1985.

Pop-Up Safety, Price Stern, 1983.

Seymour, Peter, *Playtime, Worktime*, Betty Fraser, illus., New York: Greenwillow, 1984.

Vandrell, C.S., and Parramon, J.M., *Summer*, Chicago, IL: Children's, Press, 1981.

Zokeisha, *Things I Like to Play With*, New York: Simon and Schuster, 1981.

We are happy that

_____
child's name

has been a part of

_____
name of preschool

_____
dates

_____
teacher

_____
date

"Children are an heritage of the Lord. . . ."
Psalm 127:3

We are thankful to have

_____
adult's name(s)

as a part of

_____
name of preschool

We especially recognize your efforts at:

_____

_____

_____

_____

_____
teacher

_____
date

"By the grace God has given me, I laid a foundation as an expert builder, . . ."

I Corinthians 3:10 (NIV)